Our Knickers were Interesting

Daisy Rayner

A Norfolk Village Childhood

Our Knickers were Interesting

Daisy Rayner
(1902 – 1984)

Edited by Susan Palmer

Published by Susan Palmer,
2 Elvin Road, Dereham, Norfolk NR19 2DX

ISBN 0 9515416 0 9

Designed and produced by Peter Colman Print + Design
Fakenham, Norfolk

Printed in England

Foreword

I am sure I have often said it... 'Old So-and-so has a marvellous story to tell about childhood days in Norfolk. It really ought to be put down on paper.' But it very seldom is – and alas, even if Old So-and-so does eventually get around to it, all those memories and anecdotes which sounded so fascinating around the fireside or over the bar can look painfully mundane in black and white.

But every now and again there is an exception. It may be a professional writer like Audrey Whiting or Sylvia Hayman, skilled in the use of words and capable of turning personal experiences into a good tale, so you have books like 'Gal Audrey' and 'Opposite the Cross Keys'. Far more rarely it is a country man or woman with no literary training, indeed with a minimum of general education, yet who can set down childhood memories with a clarity and simplicity that comes straight from the heart – and goes straight to the heart of the reader.

Daisy Rayner was one of these very rare people. I am sad to use the past tense, because I would have liked very much to know her. Actually our paths may have crossed during the 1950's, when I visited Swanton Morley on my reporting duties for the 'Dereham and Fakenham Times', but I cannot recall her. No matter: it is easy to imagine her talking as one reads this book, with the help of Susan Palmer's sympathetic editing, and I feel now that I know her very well.

And what an amazingly clear image she conjures up of a way of life in Norfolk which was so primitive, and so feudal, that it is difficult to believe we still live in the same century. Daisy's remarkable memory for incidents and people, her keen eye for detail, and her deep knowledge of country ways brings it all back to life – a simple, hard working, often hand-to-mouth existence where a family of ten, including three crippled children, lived in a tiny four-roomed cottage on a diet of cod's heads or boiled shinbone and yeast dough (the original Norfolk dumpling) with fried pig's belly as a treat.

Sanitation has never been Norfolk's most attractive feature. In the 'fifties we were still using a metal bucket down the garden, emptied weekly by the night-soil men – not at night but, disconcertingly, at breakfast-time. Even today many villages, like mine, lack main drainage and have to rely at best on septic tanks. But in Daisy's day the open cesspit under the 'petty' was emptied only once a year, by ladling it into buckets and pouring it into a more distant hole. Daisy had nightmares about trying to use the adults' seat instead of the smaller one for children, and falling throught the hole...

Everyone washed outside, winter and summer, in rainwater collected from the roof, with the luxury of one bath a week in a tin tub by the kitchen fire. Evenings after school for Daisy were devoted to household chores, from scrubbing the front doorstep – an emblem of respectability even in deepest Norfolk – to breaking up chunks of salt with a rolling-pin. At fourteen she went off to Dereham to work for twelve hours a day at a dressmaker's for a shilling a week, only visiting home at weekends.

It was a time when a farm worker could lose his job and his home without notice or any redress, when women and children laboured in the fields alongside their menfolk, and when the squire could order a new farmhouse to be re-positioned because it spoiled his view. But it was also a time when villagers would lay straw in the street so that a sick neighbour was not disturbed by the noise of horses and carts; when children amused themselves happily for hours with nothing more than a skipping rope or a home-made top; and when the whole family went to chapel together at least twice every Sunday, as a matter of course.

Daisy tells the story of her frugal childhood without any bitterness or complaint. 'We had a wonderful contented home life although my parents had no money. My father never did hit one of us children...' There is much of the gentle humour which is never far from the surface in Norfolk, and occasionally a reminder of the broad accent and obscure expressions which are now in danger of disappearing. 'Wha's that little ol' mawther blarring for, then?' 'Why, she only now jammed into a cow's tad!' You may have to consult the glossary to realise that the Sunday School treat was held in a field where cows had recently grazed, and Daisy had stepped unwarily, with tearful results...

There are not many tears shed in these bravely-written pages, but sometimes there is a simple statement, little more than a throw-away line, which bring home the sadness that must have been part of Daisy's life. She writes with great affection of her crippled younger brother Ben, who dragged himself around by propping his arms on a stool and using it as a makeshift crutch; she carried him upstairs to bed until he grew much bigger than she was. 'He always had a lovely smile. Even when he was dying he smiled, three times in the evening and again when I was alone with him in the morning he smiled, although he was unconscious...'

'Our Knickers Were Interesting' is an eye-catching title, and certainly Daisy's knickers were curiously constructed, but this book goes far beyond the vagaries of Edwardian underwear. It is an observant, honest account of an era which will soon be beyond living memory, seen through the eyes of a God-fearing country girl who never forgot her roots and died in the village where she was born. I have no doubt that social historians will welcome it as an authentic record of rural life in the early years of this century. But I shall treasure it as just – Daisy Rayner's story.

John Timpson

Wellingham, Norfolk.
1989

Preface

I first met Daisy Rayner in 1954 when I came as a family doctor to Dereham and its surrounding villages. She was then a busy middle-aged woman living with her husband in a low-ceilinged, tilt-floored house in Swanton Morley. Living with them were two of her crippled siblings – Ella, usually sewing – and Ben, the adored youngest child in the Beevis family, always with a beam on his face and always ready to laugh at any little story.

The crippled members of Daisy's family all had the same peculiar congenital deformity of the legs, which were more or less normal above the knee, but tapered away below. When I knew them Ella was in a wheelchair and Fred and Ben got about on their knees with short crutches.

Daisy was born in Swanton Morley in 1902 and spent her whole life there. She had no children and used her surplus energy in making things for bazaars – there was always a pile of rather old-fashioned hand-made handkerchief sachets, tea cosies, knitted dolls, etc., kept tucked away for the next Methodist bazaar. Often, if I called in the afternoon, there would be a village child on a stool near Daisy's chair being fed home-made cake and tea until his mother could call for him in the gap after school.

As she got older and physically less active Daisy's only grumble was that she couldn't help people as she was used to doing and, in the end, that she couldn't get to her beloved Chapel. It was then that I suggested she should recall her memories of what, to her, were very happy old days; very hard working, very frugal, but where you were secure in the love of your family and always prepared to help a neighbour in distress.

Daisy left school at fourteen but she told me she was 'always rather good at composition' and you will see that this was an understatement. Her whole story is told in a gentle Norfolk accent, with no pretence throughout it. The kind, bustling, never criticising person that was Daisy Rayner clearly comes through. Above all she was quite without envy, content to make the most of existence in that station in life to which her Lord had called her.

Daisy always hoped her memories would one day be published. She died in 1984 and her husband two years later.

Profits from this volume will go to a charity to be called DAISY'S MITE, to run in tandem with Small's Charity, which, under William Small's will of 1654, provides help in starting their careers for male children born in Swanton Morley village. Daisy's Mite will also help children born in Swanton Morley, especially girls, in a similar way.

Aknowledgements

In editing this work, I would like to pay tribute particularly to Mr Ivan Emson, who has done all the transcribing and who, with Mrs Richenda Wilkinson, has given much help with the editing. Mrs Pat Brudenell is also to be thanked for agreeing to deal with correspondence.

I am very much indebted to Mr John Timpson for writing a sympathetic foreword.

I would also like to thank a great many villagers of Swanton Morley – Mr Les Allcock and his mother and Mrs Connie Canham, who have given hours of their time to bring the village alive for me; Miss Edna Hilton who lent me her grandmother's cookery notebook; Mrs Ivy Pearce for Mrs Golding's medical card; Mrs Doris Cade, Mr Alan Smith and Mr Frank Davidson for photographs; and all the many, many others who have helped me, but are too numerous to mention individually.

My thanks go to Mr Leslie Allwood for his willing help and counsel on legal matters and to Mr Cyril Jolly for his advice on publishing; also to the Trustees who have kindly agreed to administer Daisy's Mite.

I would specially like to mention Daisy's relatives who have given their blessing to this publication of her work, in particular Major Daphne Beevis of the Salvation Army.

Susan Palmer
Dereham
1989

Our Knickers were Interesting

I will try and record the industry and people of Swanton Morley as I knew them in the early nineteen hundreds. Some parts may be drab and some funny. To do so I shall have to record quite a bit of myself, so I will start right at the beginning of my life.

I arrived into the family of Ellen and Alfred Beevis on September 29th 1902 and was named Daisy Alexandra. They already had five children, Herbert, Claude, Fred, William and Ella; two of these were born cripple, Fred and Ella. They had two more children later, both cripple ones. One of these died.

Daisy's parents, Ellen and Alfred Beevis.

THE HOUSE

We lived in a four-roomed cottage, the end one of a row of three. This house had a small, long kitchen, a square front room, as it was called, one large bedroom and a lean-to one. At the end of the kitchen was the fireplace, with the oven one side of it and the copper at the other side. These took up the complete end of the room. The flues went into the main chimney. The oven and the copper had separate furnaces for heating them. All waste material was burned in the copper. The fireplace itself was built up each side about eighteen inches with bricks, and had an iron grate to hold the coal or wood. There was a wooden surround and mantleshelf for small ornaments and the brass candlesticks. A buttonhook hung on a nail underneath it, and a shoehorn. The hake, which was an iron bar across the chimney, built in, was to hang the old black iron boilers and the kettle on. It had large hooks at three levels to regulate the heat. We still have the old black boilers, and I will mention them later on. The kettle was always on the hob too. As it was used on the fire it was always sooty at the back, but always had two shiny cheeks at the front away from the fire, for when the stove was polished each morning with Zebra polish the brush was rubbed over the front of the kettle, which was also an iron one. It contained a cockle shell on a piece of white knitting cotton. This was to stop fur collecting inside because the water was very hard.

From the kitchen one went into a hall about one-and-a-half yards square. The front door was here, opposite the straight open staircase. This hall led into the front room. The pantry was in here. It was rather large and it held the milk pans and cream pot, the meat safe and all food and home-made stout.

Going back to the stairs you only had to go up two or three and you could see all over the big bedroom and under the beds. The walls of this room, the two outside ones, were covered all the winter months with a greeny-black mould which was so sticky it couldn't be removed until the spring winds blew in to dry it. I remember my mother saying 'Dad, you will have to do something about the girls' bed, the mattress near the wall is quite mouldy'. From then on a thick board was fitted into the iron bedstead down by the wall. The three-quarter size bed fitted into the space between the chimney and the outside wall. My sister and I slept here. Our mother and father slept in a double bed at the centre of the opposite wall, and my youngest brother, Ben, on a put-up bed on the small landing which was a continuation of the bedroom. Later on my mother decided to make this room a little more private by having a lino and lath screen put round the stairs. From an auction she bought a huge oak screen and fixed round our bed but we still had a little space between that and the wall so we could see out of the window if we knelt on the bed. Before the screen was put round the stairs one day my mother was ill and Doctor Howlett had to be called in. He believed in fresh air. He muttered about the window being shut and at once opened it. What happened? It was a windy day and all loose things went blowing over the banister and down the stairs, for he had left the bottom door open. I remember mother hanging on to the bedclothes.

Now the boys' room – it was at the top of the stairs off the open landing. One had to go down a step to it. It had one very high wall and one very low, so at the side of the room near the window one had to bend. This room had rafters with a big beam running across, so if you used the double bed as a trampoline, I at least could get my hands over the beam and swing. I expect the boys did too. In this room was a double bed and two single ones with just a table, wash-basin and jug. It was the only private room in the house. As a little one I wondered why my mother shut herself in here, but it was the only place in which she could wash and change privately. We had two or three orange boxes made into bedside tables for they had three compartments to house our shoes and socks and small treasures. They were covered all over with wallpaper to make them pretty, and a wood beading round three sides of the top to stop safety-pins and brooches falling off.

Even with this small amount of sleeping space we had visitors to stay in the summer. They would use our parents' bed who would sleep on a mattress on the floor downstairs. Some of them would stay a fortnight or even longer. It was like this, my father was one of a family of sixteen. During a period when work was short they went away to find work and so they were dispersed all over the country; but they liked to come back to visit the old people. Their parents already had a daughter and a son-in-law living with them and the family, so the company had to stay with us.

Let's go back to the kitchen. It had a long table with a wooden form behind it near the wall. This was for us to sit at the table for meals. There were two wooden armchairs and another small one. The small one was not to sit on but for little people to wash their hands – it held an enamel bowl. Just inside the door was the important flour bin. It was as high as the table but when the lid was lifted it had two compartments for flour. This commodity was bought in ten-stone sacks, not white bags but just sacks. On the flour bin stood the litle iron sewing machine. In the corner was a fitted cupboard where plates, salt and pepper and such items were stored in the top; in the bottom half boots, dusters, polishes were kept, but if the boots were left too long they went green mouldy all over. A rag hearth-rug was in front of the fireplace, the other part of the floor was naked bricks except where one walked. These places were covered, as all cottage floors were, with corn sacks, but mother dyed hers with Condy's Fluid crystals made up with hot water in an old tin bath; they came out a lovely brown. Later, as we were able, we made other rag rugs. The floor was scrubbed twice a week. The best room had a lino square on the floor leaving one-and-a-half feet naked tiles round the walls. This room also had a rag hearth-rug. The lino was wiped over every week with a paraffin rag to preserve it. We made these rag rugs during the winter evenings. They used up the old clothes by cutting them into strips and again into three inch by three-quarter inch pieces. These pieces were pegged into hessian sugar bags which could be bought from the grocer for threepence or sixpence. We had a special tool to make the rug.

THE PETTY

The house itself was surrounded on three sides by a high bank. The road passed between our garden and one high bank so the garden was very warm. Right at the bottom of the garden was a chicken house and run, then a pig's house and then the petty. This was a small brick building about forty or fifty yards from the house. It really was a pantomime act to go there in the winter evenings. First we had to change from slippers to boots, then put hats and coats on and arm ourselves with a candle lantern which had horn windows, one of which was broken, a sad thing on windy nights, and we had to supply ourselves with a box of matches. I always went with my sister and youngest brother because they were now walking on crutches and if they couldn't see where to put their crutches at each step then they fell. The petty had two wooden seats like boxes, one low for children and one for adults, side by side. I was terrified of being lifted on to the big one when I was very small. I always had a fear that my feet and legs would go up, for it was a distance from the ground for little people to look down at. Yes, I was afraid that my legs would go up and that I should double up in the middle and slip through the hole. It must have left an impression on my mind for I have dreamed just hundreds of times about funny toilets – moveable ones, some on the market and some with the doors wide open when people were passing, some up step-ladders and in all the most ridiculous places. I still dream of them even now.

The petty had a sloping shelf you could see if you peered into the hole. You could see the cesspool too, partly inside and partly out. The outside part was covered by a few lengths of wood laid across. I remember tip-toeing across them – I wasn't very old, I didn't know then what the grey bubbly matter was beneath me. I'm glad I didn't fall in and drown in it. I was in there – in the petty – one dark night when I heard quite a noise outside and taking my lantern I went outside. Up against the wall we kept an old copper. In this was stored all the old shin bones, waiting until the man came round to buy them. A lid was kept on top but it had a hole in the side. I lifted the lid and there were three huge rats inside. I very gently put the lid back and a trap was set later.

The cesspool was only emptied once a year when the crops had been taken off the garden. A huge hole was dug and then, on a bright moonlight night, my father and another person emptied it. First it had to be ladled out with a jet – this was a hand cup or galvanized bowl on a long handle – put into pails and taken to the hole in the garden. We were always warned not to make a mistake and run over it after the soil had been put on top to cover it. Our neighbours were posh – they had a bucket in theirs, and it was across the yard opposite their door. Being old a friend emptied theirs weekly. As they were in the middle house this had to be carried over our doorstep. The man used to come to the door each Saturday and say 'Will you shut your window Ma'am and keep your door shut Ma'am'.

WASHING

To wash ouselves was even worse. Every working man's house had a solid wooden bench outside the back door and on it was an enamel bowl and soap dish with a slop pail underneath. People were very lucky who had a porch, for their bowl was under cover. Everyone washed here, winter and summer, rain or snow. The water for washing was rain washed from the roof into tubs. Day after day in the winter ice had to be broken before one could wash and lumps of ice would float in the bowl. My mother took water to the bedroom for us two girls to wash because my sister couldn't creep outside and the other two cripples had a bowl on a chair in the kitchen. During the day I had to wash outside, as well as the others. Oh! the chapped hands and the chilblained fingers we had and men had deep cracks in their hands. The three cripples had chilblains from their knees to their ankles all winter. These had to be dressed night and morning and bound with white linen covered with zinc ointment. This was a heart-breaking time for them and my mother, for the linen would stick to the raw places. I have seen them shake with dread at such times and when they were very bad I have heard her say there was proud flesh in them, and to combat this she used to rub two lumps of sugar together and let the powder drop in.

 To go back to the washing arrangements. Well, my mother had an idea. She collected a wooden box from somewhere; wooden boxes were plentiful in those days and my brothers made a wash-box to stand in the kitchen. Now every one of us could wash under cover if we abided our time. When it rained very hard every available bucket, bath or anything which would hold water was used to catch the rain when the tubs were running over. I didn't remember when the old people bathed but afterwards I thought 'Oh! my mother used to stay from chapel on Sunday afternoons' for then she had the whole house to herself.

The three youngest of us were bathed in a tin bath in front of the kitchen fire on Saturday nights. The water was heated in the copper. Mother washed us and Father dried us and put our nightdresses on. And then began the hair drill. Camphor and borax were melted in hot water and our heads were sponged and then combed with a small-tooth comb to make sure we were not farming any livestock. After this our hair was done up in pieces of rag which we called dodmans so that it would look nice on Sundays. The night before being Friday it was liquorice powder night. This was brought to us in bed and the struggle my father had with my sister was something really to remember. He would nip her nose to make her open her mouth, but she was mostly the winner and her portion went out of the window so mother wouldn't know. Another medicine we had was sulphur and treacle. This was to clear up the spots on our skin.

WATER

Our drinking water came from a well just outside the back door. Six families had to use this. I can remember it being converted into a pump by a firm called Barnham of Walsingham. And what a pump it was! One nearly always had to pour some water in before one could get any out. Sometimes water was put in because the suction tongue was dry and in winter boiling water had to be put in because it was frozen. Sometimes it packed up altogether. Then we had to get permission to go to the blacksmith's well across the road because the properties belonged to two different landlords. Quite often pails would get lost down the wells and when several people had lost them someone would borrow creepers to recover them. I don't know who these creepers belonged to, but on a Sunday morning, for that was the only spare time they had, the men would gather round the well and drop the creepers and drag the bottom for pails. I have seen them get as many as five pails out in one morning. The creeper was an iron with three curved arms, like an umbrella upside-down.

In very dry weather we had to go down the road to the sluice, which was at the bend in Town Street. There was a straight wall with steps down each side of it and, behind it, a square brick well where one could dip the pail, and however empty it became at night it would be full again by morning. This is now buried under the road. If the dry weather continued too long, and it did sometimes for I have seen cabbages turn blue with the dry and the heat, then I have seen my father put a tub on the tumbril and go down to the river for water for the animals to drink. This water was a mile away.

SELF-SUFFICIENCY

Quite early in my life the family had two cows. It was quite common for people to keep them. Dick Spelman had one, John Hudson had some, Walter Bone, Nipper Anderson and Phillip Pegg, I remember all those having them. During the summer these were fed by the roadside. Phillip Pegg who lived the farthest from the common would collect them on his way down Mill Street or Miller's Lane, and let them feed on the sides of the road. After school our boys and others would go and collect them. I have often been during the holidays with a boy next door to collect them and let them feed on the way home. My mother became too overworked to milk ours and make butter, so they were sold and two bullocks bought each autumn to fat in the winter. We had pigs in the summer. Father hired a row of buildings separate to the house.

The house rent was five pound a year payable at Michaelmas. We always had a pony and cart because my father hired about five acres of allotment in different parts of the village. He worked this land after working all day, but his day was not as long as the land worker for he worked on Bylaugh Hall golf course and he would be coming home from work as we came out of school. Walter Bone did most of the ploughing for all the allotment holders, they paid him by the acre. Father's wages were seventeen shillings a week when the land workers' wages were twelve and six. I realize now they must have been almost self-supporting. We, like nearly everyone, kept some chickens and rabbits and sometimes ducks. These were never sold but were kept for eating. We always reared chicks under broody hens in small coops in the summer. Now no backyard hens laid eggs during the winter months, so when they did lay, starting about February, the surplus eggs were put into pails of waterglass and kept for cooking or frying.

Most of the vegetables were grown on the allotments. The potatoes were brought home and haled in the garden. How we younger ones hated it when the hales were opened on a sunny day in spring and all of us had to help sort them. Turnip-top salad was a favourite spring green to be used after sprouts were finished. These were obtained by laying swedes into a trench in winter and when they started to shoot in spring the shoots were pulled off, something like sprouting broc. We had a William pear tree on the house wall, a Worcester Pearmain apple and a Pompey apple tree. This was in the chicken run. I used to climb it and sit there to read in the summer. I was out of other people's way up there. We also had a Cox's apple tree planted by my brother Herbert. When he was missing, presumed killed, in the war this tree died suddenly. It was packed with apples almost ready to eat. We had a plum tree and a large bullace plum, and the bank on Spelmans' garden side was full of plum trees. The fruit was small but very sweet.

My mother preserved everything she could get to make our meals interesting. She used crab-apples, wild blackberries, little red wild plums. Bullaces and damsons we had by the stone, grown on the hedge in the allotment. During the first world war she made carrot jam and green tomato jam. She made all kinds of pickles – onion, cabbage, mustard, sweet pickle, walnuts – mushroom ketchup and a sauce like HP. I had to help with the walnuts. They were gathered in July before the shell set and we used two forks to prick them all over. Then they were put in brine for a week and then laid out on a cloth in the sun to dry and turn black before being put into vinegar.

THE DAILY ROUTINE

I must say our house was kept clean, for after the rooms were cleaned and beds made we had to give a very good reason for going in the front room or upstairs. Now let's go back to the kitchen for this is where the family were kept happy and clean. Mostly on Mondays mother would tidy up the house because we used the big room on Sundays. She brushed and cleaned all the Sunday clothes and put them away in drawers and boxes. Once a month father would say 'Don't put my hat away today for it's parish council meeting tonight'. He was on the council for many years. Letters were also written on Monday mornings. Tuesday was washday. The copper had to be filled with rainwater from the tubs outside the back door. If the water was getting low it had to be strained through muslin because it would be full of little wiggly, squiggly things. A round wooden tub was used to wash the clothes in, but first the fire under the copper had to be lit and when the water was warm enough all clothes had to be hand-washed. Some people had rubbing boards and just one or two had a dolly tub. This was a deep tub, and a little wooden stool on a tall handle which was turned backward and forward. After they were hand-washed they were boiled, brought out of the copper and rubbed again. There was quite a lot of boiling for we wore white calico chemises, drawers, nightdresses and white aprons. They had to be put through several waters – blue water, and then starch water for aprons and pinafores.

What a trouble to get things dry in those days! Sometimes they hung out all the week in winter, for they were wrung by hand. Later we had an old wringer with wooden rollers. This was so large it had to stand in an open-fronted shed in the garden. It was bought at an auction. Our old neighbour had had one for years and people would bring her a basketful of clothes to mangle, for which she charged one penny. There was an old lady, Mary Pegg, who had one of the very old type. It took up a large part of her room. It was a huge box-like affair. The clothes were all folded and put in, then they were weighed down with a box of huge stones. It had chains and pulleys to lift this box of stones up and down. I never did see it being worked, although she called me in to look at it one day.

Ironing was a trying time too, especially in hot weather, for a huge fire had to be made up to heat the irons in the centre. These irons were then taken out when red hot and put into an iron-box. Every little while one had to change them for another so the fire was disturbed all the time. Some people used flat-irons. These were heated on the top of the fire but they were so rough they had to be put into a metal shoe. One house where they took washing in had a square stove in the middle of the room, the chimney pipe going up, then across and through the outside wall. This stove had two ledges round where flat-irons would be heated.

Mens' shirts were very hard to wash for they were made from Oxford shirting with grey calico lining half-way down the fronts and backs. They didn't have Sunday shirts, they only had collar-bands on the shirts for, for working, they wore neckerchiefs, and for Sundays white starched fronts and collars were worn. These were fixed on with collar studs. There was always the stamping round of feet to get these on, for the button-holes were too stiff to open. Mens' winter underwear were also hard to wash and dry for they were fleecy-lined.

Wednesdays and Saturdays were baking days. Everyone had to make their own bread for there were no bakers' carts coming round then though I do remember the very first bread brought round to the door later. How beautiful the house smelled on days when the bread was baked, and little crusty loaves for us children to have opened up and butter put in while they were still hot. The flour was put into an earthenware vessel and the dough made at night, covered with a white cloth and a cushion. In the morning our huge bowl would be full and sometimes hanging over the side.

When the oven or copper flue was blocked a teaspoonful of gunpowder was wrapped in a wad of newspaper, pushed into the furnace and the door shut hastily and pushed tight with a poker until one heard a big boom. I have done this, and have bought the gunpowder from the ironmonger's. The oven was a box-like affair let into the wall. It was made of iron with a cast iron floor below it. These ovens had three brass knobs – one for opening the door and two to clear the soot off the flue at the top. Sometimes the sides would burn out and then a bricklayer had to come and take it out and it was sent to the blacksmith's to be re-bodied. What a mess it made, for sometimes the gaping hole was open for days and no fire could be lit in the grate.

FOOD

I was going to talk about the food which was cooked on Saturdays but for this I must go back to Thursday, for this is when the butcher delivered the meat for the week-end. We always had a piece of best brisket on the bone – this was cooked on Saturdays for us to have a cold lunch on Sundays – and a whole shin-bone and small piece of shin. After the war we had a complete shin-bone with all the meat on. Now the old boilers which I have spoken of came into use. They stood on the kitchen hobs from now on until Saturday morning boiling the shin-bone and the brisket and being replenished with hot water when needed. Saturdays it was strained and allowed to get cold. It set a thick jelly. Then the marrow was taken off and used later during the week for dripping toast. Next our Sunday morning breakfast was prepared in a very large oblong dish. After the brisket was cooked the gravy was mixed with the jelly and salt and pepper, and to make it brown and give it flavour a level tablespoonful of white sugar was put into an iron spoon and held in the oven furnace until it bubbled and bubbled and turned almost black. This was

Daisy's mother making pastry.

then added to the mixture. The piece of shin already cooked was put in the end of the dish for my father's breakfast and the boys' if they wanted it. The dish was then put back into the oven to boil up again.

On Sunday mornings we had thick slices of bread put on our plates and spoonfuls of jelly put on top. We ate this with pickle cabbage vinegar. Any jelly left would be made into soup. I remember one brother coming home on leave. He said he hoped there would be jelly for breakfast for he had thought about it in the trenches. We were away one Sunday and the three boys had this big dish on the table instead of the brisket when Doctor Howlett called. He told my mother afterwards that he got wrong with his wife over this because he told her poor people lived better than they did.

Saturday mornings when I was old enough I was sent to the butcher's for threepennyworth of pieces. These were scraps taken from the bones and awkward pieces (today they are rolled up in the joints). My mother made these pieces and others cut from the brisket into a hot-pot for Saturday tea – the men worked all day Saturdays – and for a sweet we mostly had potato and suet cakes with deep criss-crossed marks on the top. They were baked until they were quite a dark brown and then split open and served with treacle. We all wanted top pieces. While talking about Saturdays I will mention Alice who used to come and play with us. She had no young brothers and sisters at home so she liked to stay and eat with us at mid-day. If she was there mother would give me a penny and say 'Run down to the shop when Alice isn't looking and get a tin of potted meat'. The penny tin would be about the size of a cotton reel and would make sandwiches for three or four of us.

The meat in the week was horrible for we had sheep's head and pluck. I presume the pluck was the lungs or lights. We didn't eat this, although the neighbours did. Sometimes we had half bullock's heads – what tales those old boilers could tell of chattering teeth! The heads were cleaned and the eyes taken out. Oh-er! how I hated to see those great jaw-bones and teeth being taken out. Of course they were taken away before they came to table. Meat left from the meal was used in other ways – some minced, mixed with breadcrumbs, herbs and eggs and made into a meat roll and used when cold. I liked this. When hot we had suet dumpling or Norfolk dumpling served with the head. Norfolk dumpling was yeast dough taken from the bread dough. We had half pig's heads. These were made into pork cheese, known in other places as brawn. I have watched the process many a time and even the ears were scraped both sides to get the most off it. The meat was chopped after the bones were taken out and nutmeg and salt and pepper added, and a spoonful of white sugar burned as for the Sunday breakfast jelly. This was my mother's secret. The butcher, William Bone, would have loved to know how she got them brown and shining.

We should have been brainy really for we had cods heads too. These were served with lots of white sauce and bread and butter. A small piece of cod was bought with the head for the working men. Sometimes on Tuesdays we had a pound and a half of pig's fry but this was difficult to serve being heart, liver and fat. We had pigs bellies (chitterlings), but not often for most people liked these and the pig only had one, didn't it? We used to take a pail for this, not to the butcher but to the grocer. He had pigs killed in buildings at the back of the shop. The butcher too killed all his meat at the back of the butcher's shop in Greengate. We collected the whole lot, the belly and what the pig had eaten before it was killed. Now two people had to clean this. First it was pulled apart and some of the fat taken off. Then the fun began. My mother used to stretch her fingers in one end and my sister or I would pour water in and with her other hand mother would squeeze down the belly to get the dung out. It was then turned inside-out and put into salt water and each day it had to be cleaned and turned for about a week and more fat taken off. When really cleaned it was boiled and when cold, fried.

Another food we had in season was lamb's tails. Ooh horrible! The lamb's tails had to be taken off for they grew so long and if they got coated with mud they would drag the lambs down and once they got down on their back, sheep or lambs, they couln't get up again and would die. My grandfather and uncle were both shepherds so we had some each year. Once was enough for me. The wool had to be pulled off and then they were scalded to get the hairs off, boiled and put into lamb's-tail pie. My mother used to do some of these and pigs' bellies and send to an uncle in London.

We also had eels. A friend of my father's lived by the river. These had to be skinned alive and would even move in the frying-pan. For a sweet pudding we had suet puddings with syrup, plum duff, boiled batters, apple puddings. Most puddings were boiled in a cloth, like jam roly-polies.

WORK

The first thing I can really remember was standing in the yard holding my mother's hand. It was a breezy morning and I heard her say 'They're going to grind corn today – I can hear the sails beginning to turn on the mill', which was on the hill just above us. Another morning when the womenfolk stood in the yard after watching the children go to school I heard them say 'Just listen, someone is dead'. The sexton had to toll the church bell for an hour, pulling it once, twice or three times before resting. This was to let the village know someone had died and to let them know if the someone was a male, a female or a child.

I'm going on a few years. My brother Herbert was the oldest and he had a job on the land. The land was his life – he loved it. Claude left school next. He couldn't get work at once so John Craske offered him a job going round on his fish cart and at his shop. Claude was too particular for this job, he couldn't bear the fish smell or the messiness of it, so in time he went on the land. When Billy left school he went as a cowman.

The day started very early in our house, for whatever time of year it was the sticks which had been drying in the hearth all night had to be lit in the grate before anyone could have a cup of tea. This was my father's job in the week, but mother did it Sunday mornings. To help the fire blaze, cold cinders were put in a jar and paraffin added. Or you could buy a square piece of pumice stone with a wire fixed through it and do the same with this. I said an early start in the mornings because the boys had to be at work at six-thirty and they had a mile to walk. No cycles then! They started work at seven o'clock in the winter.

There were dinners to pack for Herbert, Claude and my father. Billy came home as cowmen had two hours at mid-day. He was a milker and had to work later in the day.

There was no white paper at that time, if there was I cannot remember it; no food boxes either, so red handkerchiefs were used. The food was stacked in the

The windmill and the church, 1914.
The little boy on the left with the crutches is Daisy's brother Fred.

middle of one of these and taking three corners one gave a little flick and tied the other corner round. The red handkerchiefs had three different designs and three different sizes. They were the handkerchief, the tommy handkerchief (tommy meaning food) and the neckerchief used round the neck. The food and drink were then put into frail baskets – these were made of rushes and had an oblong lid which a handle passed through. The basket had two rush bands round it. The men added two leather straps where they put their arms through and then the basket rested across their backs.

For drink they took cold tea, no milk or sugar. A bottle was put in each end of the basket to balance it. We had a large jug standing on the flour bin and every drop of tea left over was drained into this every time tea was made. I don't think tea could have been used very long for a neighbour used to send me to the shop for two ounces which was weighed into newspaper. She said she bought it in ounces so she could get a down scale every time. She forgot she had to have the weight of the newspaper each time as well.

THE CRIPPLES

After the workers had left home there was room for us younger ones to get dressed. Ben, the youngest, was already down for he was always first and you can imagine, while four people were getting ready for work he would get in their way for he had to creep around. So in time as he heard the others on the stairs he would roll himself underneath the couch and when any of them said 'Where's the little brat this morning?' he would poke his head out and grin up at them. He always had a lovely smile, even when he was dying he smiled, three times in the evening and again when I was alone with him in the morning he smiled although he was unconscious.

I suppose Fred and Ella had to learn to get about the same as he did, but they were older than I so I don't know how they started. I do know how Ben started to walk. We had a home-made wooden stool. Every household had them for children to sit on. This one was not very high. He used to raise himself up with this, move it a little way and then drag his body along. He used this way to get about after he started school. Ella, my sister, did the same on her last journey from my living room down the passage to her bedroom, only she hadn't the strength to move the stool so I moved it for her and she dragged her body up to it each time.

My brother Ben I carried up the stairs for years until he was much bigger than me. I feel horrified when I think back, for we had no handrail and he became so heavy that I couldn't hold him on at all. He only hung on with his arms round my neck. My hands had to grip the edges of the stairs and when I was two steps from the top I would half turn and shoot him up onto the landing where he would just lay on his back and laugh.

Ben.

Our parents used to have crutches made for these three by Monument Brothers of Dereham. Fred, who was not so bad, had broom-handles with shaped arm-pieces at the top. The others, both pairs, were split with a handle in the centre. They had a metal ring at the bottom and when slippery a rubber shoe was put on over it. These cost ten shillings a pair. The crutches wore their clothes out very quickly and perfectly good clothes were patched under the arm. As the patches wore they were taken off and other patches put on. For this reason they were allowed extra clothing coupons during the Second World War.

CLOTHES

Our clothes were mostly hand made from someone else's left-offs, made by my mother and Mrs Mace, a neighbour. She had been trained as a dressmaker. Mother used to sit up at night to do this sewing for she made all the underclothes and the mens' shirts. She used a small iron machine and I can remember the village policeman saying to her 'I'm coming round to your house one night to see what you are doing, for yours is always the last light to go out in the village'. I've heard her say that she always watched the clock to make sure it didn't strike after she got upstairs, so if father woke he wouldn't know what time she had gone to bed.

With all this sewing I can only remember having four really new frocks until I made them myself. After Claude went in the army his Sunday coat was made into one for me. The first new frock I can remember well for it was black. My grandfather had left a golden half sovereign for each of his grand-children to buy their mourning. My sister's and mine were black figured alpaca. These frocks were made by Miss Flo Smith. We had huge cream hats; the crowns were almost like chamber-pots. These were trimmed with black ribbon. Going into black was a must for a funeral, even as far as using black-bordered handkerchiefs and envelopes. These the housewife dreaded.

Widows had to wear widow's weeds. They wore small hats which were draped with crape, not crepe, then hung down the back like a person wears a jabot in the front of a blouse today. She had to wear these and black clothes for six months and then she could gradually get back to colours by first wearing purple then mauve for another three months. Men who were only slightly related could wear black arm-bands. Most women went into black when their parents died and kept in black for the rest of their lives because when people got to that stage other members would be dying and they couldn't afford new clothes for them all.

Let me go back to my other dresses. My next one was a grey alpaca. This was when my brother was presumed dead in the First World War. Then I had a new white one, when girls of my age had new dresses to be confirmed in. And the nice one I can see being made now. I would be about eleven years old. It was green and honey-brown dog-tooth check. It was a very wet day when I went in from school, the fire was blazing and the oil lamp lit, and there sat my mother stitching away with her little hand machine. My new dress! The old clock, which we still have, was ticking away behind her and the kettle boiling on the hob.

Our underwear was all home-made from calico or long-cloth, as were the nightdresses. These were mostly made in the evenings for this kept hands from getting into mischief. How many times did I hear that 'The devil finds mischief for idle hands to do'. The chemises were huge affairs made magyar style – the whole width of the material with extra pieces put in the sides. The neck was cut extra large and then gathered into a one-and-a-quarter inch band. The gathers had to be pulled up tight first and then stroked so that they could be worked along evenly. The band had narrow torchon lace at the edge and was feather-stitched. Nightdresses had yokes and were open a little way down like a man's shirt – I now realize that men's shirts open all the way down today, but they didn't then – with about five tucks each side of the opening. We were taught to do tucks in school by first drawing a thread of the material out and putting running stitches in the place.

Our knickers were interesting. They were open part of the way down the sides. The front half stitched into a band which did up at the back with two buttons. The back had a short band and was buttoned at the sides. In this way you could drop the back like the tail-board of a cart, only these were held up with buttons and not with chains! Elastic was only used to hold hats on with, the elastic went under the chin. Wide elastic was used on gaiters to go under the feet. Adult ladies wore shaped bands about three and a half inches wide with just two calico legs joined on. They were made by overlapping the legs at the front and buttoning the band over at the back. Both these and the children's were gathered into a three-quarter inch band near the bottom of the legs to form a frill. The ladies' legs were almost down to the ankle.

We wore black wool worsted stockings and boots and, in winter, gaiters made of thick black material. These and ladies' boots were buttoned, the buttons being on the outside of the leg. I think when I see zipped-up boots today someone have made a mistake and put them in the wrong side. Because these buttons were small and round, one had to use a button-hook to fasten them – not an easy performance when one was in a hurry. We were taught in school to re-feet the stockings by cutting away the underpart of the foot. We cut a piece off from another old stocking about an inch bigger than this and ran it all round, then herring-boned it down to make it flat. I never wore any done like this.

Older people wore two or three petticoats gathered into bands at the waist. The real old people wore shawls in summer and thick capes for winter, and small bonnets. Gloves had buttons and button-holes as well. For working in the morning women mostly wore coloured aprons or, for cooking, a large starched white one, but if they did washing, washing floors or dirty work then they wore a sacking apron. This was always worn for anything rough. Every day after dinner my mother washed and changed before we came home from school.

OUTSIDE

I will continue now from the outside of the house. Just past the bench where we washed was a coal shed, known as the shud. It was back to the kitchen so the wall behind the fireplace was warm, and working coats hung here. At the furthest from the door the coal and wood were stored with a rack above to store tools which were used in season, such as rakes and hoes and hooks and things which were not in continual use. It also housed the now disused butter churn. It was a square box-like affair. I cannot remember seeing it used. When visiting an uncle on the farm at North Tuddenham his churn was quite different – more barrel type.

Just across the yard from the coal shed was the cart shed. This was made with fir-tree posts at each corner. Rails were nailed to three sides of this and furze bushes were threaded into them from the bottom upwards. To do this work leather gloves had to be used. I believe this one had a galvanized roof, but the one on the allotment had layers and layers of straw and hay and then furze bushes. These sheds never got wet inside. One would find sheds and cart sheds on the farms like this and in meadows where cattle and ponies grazed, to give some protection in bad weather. They were mostly in a corner backing a high hedge, and bullock yards were divided in the same way. Across the yard was the neighbour's petty, another shed for the tumbril and a place for the bullocks or pigs, a store place for mangel and hay, and the pony's stable and the landlady's wash-house.

CHILDREN'S WORK

There was not much time to play except in the summer holidays for every child had homework to do. Not school homework – we did that while in school – but real work. As the older members of the family went out to work we had to take over their jobs. When old enough I always had to do the errands for milk and meat and apples on Saturdays. I had to scrub the front doorstep and whiten it with a brick of hearthstone and scrub the petty floor. In turn I had to chop sticks and clean knives and forks. The knives were steel and had to be rubbed on a knife board with bath brick sprinkled on. You could buy special boards, but ours was just a piece of board worn smooth by constant use. I was glad when the youngest member of the household had to take over the last two jobs, for although some of us were cripples they didn't get excused from work but had to do their share. My sister did the mending and knitting.

Other jobs we had to do were cutting newspaper into squares for the lavatory. I only saw a toilet roll when I was about fourteen years old. Even so, people were not using them in nineteen thirty-six, for a neighbour asked me then if I could let her have some off my roll because little Robert's bottom was sore.

We also had to break up salt. This was bought in half-stone blocks as hard as rock. We used to take a blunt knife and cut and knock pieces off, then with a rolling-pin and pastry board would knock and hammer it and then roll it to get the smaller lumps out. It came in newspaper, and Kingston's store in Dereham had a shed near the pavement in Norwich Street where it was stored in huge blocks. It used to come to them on an open dray on sacks and was stored on the floor and cut into lengths with a saw.

CHILDREN'S GAMES

There was not much time for games except play-time at school and on our way to and fro from school and doing errands, and during school holidays. The games came in rotation according to the time of the year. I think hoops came first. We would use these doing the errands as we did them more quickly while trundling a hoop. I used an iron one which was a left-off of my brothers. Spinning tops came in with the March dust, when the roads were dry, then marbles followed. The girls played fivestones. This was played on the barn doorstep if fine, if wet, on the petty floor – ours or our neighbour's or aunt's, whichever we fancied. Many a boy got into trouble at top time, for most of the tops were home-made from large cotton reels. These were plugged with wood and a hobnail was used for a toe for it to spin on. Hobnails were nails with rounded heads and all boys had two or three rows round the outside edge of the boots which also had iron tips at the toe and iron cleats at the heel. The boys would take a knife or something to pick a nail out of their boots, if they wanted a toe for their tops. Girls had iron protectors on the soles of their shoes. These protectors were bought in a cardboard folder, enough for one pair.

Skipping was the game I loved. I remember being in Dereham with my mother, and how I cried and cried for a skipping-rope with handles at Brenner's Stores. I knew later why she couldn't buy one, for after I was married I hadn't enough money, while shopping, to buy a cup of tea, for I was determined never to get into debt.

Harker's Lane was one of the places in which we played. There was always a donkey tethered there. To pass it we went over the hedge then back into the lane again. It would always come to meet us – I suppose the poor thing was lonely and wanted us to talk to it. We had a row of 'armchairs' up this lane. A very old hedge must have been cut down here and the stubs were allowed to grow out again. Because every child would run to sit on them first, the front didn't grow but they branched at the sides and back. Further up we had a 'couch' – two oak trees stood some distance apart and although a hedge grew the field side, nothing but fine grass grew on the flat, level side in the lane.

From the Harker's Lane hedges we used to break branches off the hazel bushes and bring them back to the school playground. A little brown insect like a beetle, which we called locusts, lived in the lime trees at the top of the hill. They used to fly out in the evenings. We would knock them down with the leafed branches just to hold them in our hands and see how many we could get. They did tickle. We never hurt them and let them all go before going home.

Later in the summer we played with pop-guns made from pieces of elder stems. The centre pith was taken out and a hazel stick was made to fit and a half acorn was put in the end for the ammunition. We got sore mouths biting acorns. Whistles were made from hemlock stems, and real good ones could be made of a young sycamore stem. Hawthorn pips were shot from a split stick. Another game was played with two sticks, a long and a short one. The short piece was lodged on a stone and hit with the long one, and as it rose up it would be hit sideways – known as chop stick. Boys would go to the shop and get a pig's bladder, take the fat off and then blow it up like a football, to play with. We played T-takem with a little square piece of wood which had letters on each side. We paid with marbles. Later we used to make a little movable toy. It was only made with cotton reels and a piece of candle and a rubber band – I forget exactly how it was made.

Summer holidays when hot and sunny, we would go up Elsing Road and lie under the huge oak trees; when tired we would lay back and listen to the hum of the insects and the birds, for there was no other sound – no aeroplanes or cars or land machine tools to make a noise. We could on a quiet evening stand in our back yard and hear the waterfall at Mill Street roaring away. From the tall grass which grew around us we used to weave bands and if near the river we would make doll's baskets with rushes. At that time there were lots of meadows for cattle, for all farmers kept cattle and horses. These would be white and yellow with buttercups and daisies, with rabbits' little white tails bobbing up here and there. With the flowers we made daisy chains and hung round our necks and held bunches of buttercups under each other's chin to see if they liked butter better than us. The banks and ditches in spring were covered with primroses and violets. We would gather them by the basketful for they grew everywhere. Easter time we used to send them to a cousin in London to decorate her church and later we sent them to a blind home in Norwich.

One of the girls' pastimes in summer was to make a 'pin to peep'. First we found a pane of glass and made an arrangement of the most colourful flower-heads we could find. We would cover these with brown paper and then about an inch from three edges we cut a straight line so there was a flap we could lift up. No-one looked inside this flap unless they gave a pin. Now pins were very plentiful, for almost everything we bought had elevenpence-three-farthings added and a packet of pins was given instead of the farthing. A very dear friend of my mother's, Granny Goward we called her, she bought something from H H Aldiss of Dereham – grandfather to the present owner. The assistant gave her pins for her farthing change but she wouldn't accept them. They told her they had no farthings in the shop, but she wouldn't leave the shop without her farthing and so in the end one of the girls had to go out and find her one. I heard her tell this tale herself and she said 'A farthing's a farthing and it's as much use to me as it is to Mr Aldiss'. I can picture her, bosom heaving and her giggle as she told us. Granny Goward's husband George was one of the Chapel Elders.

WILD FOOD

When we were on our rambles we would eat all kinds of things from the hedgerows. Fresh hawthorn leaves, we called these bread and cheese. We looked especially for young shoots on wild roses and when found them we would peel them and eat them, also the seed of the mallow we called pick-cheeses and sorrel leaves which were small green leaves close to the ground. We nibbled hips and hawses and if we were near a turnip field we would slip over the hedge and get small turnips, rub them on the grass and peel them with our teeth and eat. My brothers used to find ground nuts, but I never could. My husband say they had small leaves like a fern.

SCHOOL

My brothers and my sister and I went to the Church school in The Street, which is now the village hall. In my brothers' time Mr and Mrs Brain were the teachers, but in my time the schoolmaster and his wife were Mr and Mrs Edwin Weaver. He was a very strict and rather sharp-tempered man and many were the times he used to use the cane, mostly on our hands but on the backsides of the boys and he'd make them stand on chairs and hold up slates, and when their arms fell down he would hit them on the elbow. I remember once sitting at the end of a back row of the class. I always was a fidget with my hands. Quite unconsciously I got hold of the

Swanton Morley School Group, 1912.
Back row: *Daisy Beevis, Willie Jarrett, Mabel Jarrett, Ida Reeve, Roy Money, Bertie Large, Teacher – Miss Maggie Russell.*
Middle row: *Violet Anderson, Len Cullum, Eddie Watkins, Len Butters, Katherine Marsh, Hubert Kingsley, Percy Moore.*
Front row: *Alice Macrow, Edith Howard, Emily Anderson, Bertie Reeve, Rosie Money, Elizabeth Macrow, Edith Harrison, Alice Easter, Rosa Myhill.*

bell-rope. I was listening to the teacher when suddenly the bell rang. I was more surprised than anyone. In a minute, although he was with another class he shouted 'Who did that? Come on, out here' and I had the cane. It wasn't the cane that hurt but the disgrace in having to go in front of the class to receive it. I wonder what happened to that bell when the building was altered.

After I grew older I have often said 'Thank you' to him in my mind for all his efforts and for teaching us so well. Mrs Weaver was very kind and clever. They had a grown-up family and one young daughter. Mrs Weaver taught the infants with the aid of a young assistant, Mabel Seaman, who wanted to be a teacher. Mrs Weaver also taught all the older girls both knitting and sewing. We did socks, fancy knitting and sewing chemises, nightdresses and petticoats. In her own home she knitted long coats in Arran and cable stitch. She made them to sell and we children thought they were wonderful.

The master and his wife lived across the way at 'Homelea'. At that time the house front was black beams and white plaster, but while I was at school it was bricked over.

I have said that Mrs Weaver was kind. She would take the small children's boots and socks off and dry their winter coats when the weather was real bad. The winter coats boys wore often were ladies' left-off costume coats. The costume skirts could be worn up in the house but people couldn't wear the jackets. I followed two boys up the road one day. They did look funny, for their coats were nipped in at the waist with a little flare at the lower edge. I should think they were new that day to them. They did look pleased with themselves.

The children started school at five years old. They had to come from the farthest cottages in Hoe and from Worthing and Bylaugh Oaks. Everybody had to walk, there was no transport and none of the mothers came with them. The oldest of the family had to look after all the others, and they were not allowed to stay away, for an attendance officer came round to the schools often – a Mr Addison – and if a child was away for half a day he would visit the parents to know the reason why. Only a few years ago I met one of the boys who had a long way to come and he told me that they were hungry. They brought their dinner but often ate it on the way to school and then had to wait until night. When Mrs Weaver heard of such cases, or if some child had forgotten to bring theirs, she would provide them with food.

She taught in the small room, where there were two classes. If you look in this room today you will see that part of the floor is put in it in a different fashion. This is because in my brothers' schooltime a gallery was here. I think it was formed of tiers of seats one above another. The billiards room of today had two classes, taught by Miss Maggie Tye, whose name later was Mrs Harrold. On Thursdays all the older girls used this room for sewing. The boys on these days, if fine, would go to the allotments on the Elsing Road where each had his own portion of garden. If wet they were taught painting. The big room had three classes. Miss Maggie Russell was one teacher and the master taught the other two classes. Each room had one small fire with a high iron guard round and only once can I remember being allowed to wear our coats for lessons. The ceilings were much higher then. It was open right up to the roof. It was only after it ceased to be a school that the present ceiling was put in. Above this are some most magnificent dark oak beams.

We had lift-up desks with a rail for our backs. They had a fixed space at the front for inkwells. We used ink for exam papers and lessons which had to be marked after school, but for most of the time we had slates framed with wood and slate pencils which scratched and squeaked as we wrote. There was a square hall at each entrance to the school, one for boys and one for girls; pegs were on the walls and on the passage walls. In each hall there was a small round hand-basin with a plug, but no water, except a pailful standing by, so that those who stayed for dinner would be able to have a drink. There was one chipped enamel mug.

Now for the toilets. They were just outside the girls' door, four very narrow places for the females, the furthest for the little girls, the next two for the middle girls and the first for the teachers. They were almost back-in-and-walk-out places. I had pressing business to do there once. It must have been in the afternoon for the pails were getting full and this splashed up onto my bottom and I was horrified. I can only remember going there twice more in my schooldays and then I nipped into the teachers', hoping all the time no-one would come, and then skipped out into the next toilet to get re-arranged again. The caretaker and cleaner had to empty these every night by taking them across the road to the schoolmaster's garden and I presume burying the contents.

Once a year a caravan vehicle came to the village and was stationed in Darby's yard. After it had arrived it was cranked out to two-thirds of its size so now it was a square room. Here girls over eleven went for three week's lessons – one week cooking, one week washing and one week housewifery. I still have my book which I was given at that time.

All the walls in the school were painted pale green at the top and a very dark green shining paint at the bottom, about four feet up. In the winter little rivulets of water could be seen running down the walls. All the girls wore white or light pinafores and had long hair tied with a ribbon. One girl from a poor family had her hair tied with a bootlace, or the pink tape off new sheets. This girl had a very poor life. I shall be talking about her later on.

FRED'S APPRENTICESHIP

About the time I'm thinking of now, Fred – the oldest cripple – would be leaving school. My parents wanted him to learn a trade so that as time went on he would be able to provide for himself. They thought tailoring was the only thing he would be able to do, so they tried two or three places but no-one would take him because, they said, he would not be able to use the heavy irons for pressing. After thinking again they decided to try and make him a snob – a shoemaker. Most working men had hand-made boots and boys had them too. They tried a shoemaker at Billingford – a Mr Howard – known as 'Snobby' Howard. 'Yes, he would be pleased to learn him'. The snag was, how would he get there? They couldn't afford to board him out, so they bought a bucket-type cart known as a governess cart and they also bought him a little pony – a little fellow by the name of Tommy and so he started driving himself morning and night. Many were the anxious moments my mother had watching the clock, especially on winter evenings. I'm not sure, but I think he went there five years because he was apprenticed. Tommy was a dear little pony but he had one fault. If he felt he wanted to turn completely round in the road he'd do so and no-one, whatever they did, could make him change his mind. After Fred had finished his apprenticeship he thought he would like to start on his own. The cart shed made of furze bushes was taken down and a shepherd's hut was bought and put in its place. Here he worked for many years.

PEOPLE OF THE VILLAGE

Now I will talk about the neighbours. Next door to us lived an old couple, Dick and Amelia Spelman. He had already had a stroke and had asthma and was past work. How they provided for themselves I don't knw. He did at one time take a basket of cottons and tapes etc. around by donkey-cart, but I believe people robbed them. His hobby was to go to Pennyspot Wood and bring back great branches of wood on his shoulder. He sladed one foot, but he loved sawing wood. If the branches were big and sprawly he would drag them. It didn't matter if they filled the whole road, for he knew he wouldn't meet anything unless it was someone walking.

Dick was an old fraud really – quite a lovable one. If his wife was ill, so was he. Someone had to walk into Dereham every week to get him a bottle of medicine. It was mixed at the doctor's. These two slept in the house next to us, backing the wall where our bed was and often during the night we would hear him shout to Amelia, for she was deaf, 'Go and get her, for I'm dying' so Amelia would knock on the wall for mother. Once they got the landlady there as well. They were both watching him – he had his eyes closed. Betsy Golding said 'Come on mor, he 'on't die tonight I now see him wink'. It became such a habit of this couple that at last mother had to refuse to get up. For a time the old man didn't want to die or if he did he decided to do it without the neighbours' help.

These two kept bees, about eight hives in a kind of shelter under the edge of one of the high banks. When there was a swarm Amelia would run indoors for a big dustpan and an iron key and ting them. If she did this she could go on anyone's land and claim them. She would talk to the bees and if any member of the family died she would put a piece of black material on the hives and tell them all about it. She would walk amongst them with bare arms. When they took up the honey Dick would say 'Give her a bit, give her a bit.' He never called me by name and I would be walking along the yard with a piece of honeycomb with honey dripping everywhere. She used to make beeswax and sell it to the tailors.

The Spelmans practically lived on broth from boiled bones, and bread sop. Bread sop is bread broken into a pudding-basin, hot water poured on and a piece of butter put on the top and pepper and salt added. When babies were weaned this is what the mothers fed them on, sucking each spoonful first. All babies were breast-fed and mothers would put the baby to the breast just anywhere they were and at any time. Now Amelia and Dick had brought up a nephew and a grandson as well as their own family. In later years the daughter Amelia came home to look after them.

At the cottage at the other end of the row lived the landlady, Betsy Golding, Mr and Mrs Mace and their family, and one by the name of Lily Head – I think she was a foster-child. Betsy Golding was quite old. She loved my sister and as long as she lived she gave her a penny a week and left her five pounds in her will. She got old and deaf, but still they had to have her consent to have repairs done to the cottage.

Because the old landlady lived there we were not allowed to bounce balls on any wall and neither was my father allowed to sweep the chimney, so in summer we had the sweep to do the chimneys for us. But they wanted doing twice a year, so just before Christmas father would do it in the evening when it was dark. He used a bunch of holly tied to canes with binder string – not rods but just garden canes. One year it went wrong. He pushed it above the pot – and this particular one had points all round the top – and there the holly remained for weeks.

Now we'll go down the yard and round the corner. Here was an old barn which had been used in its time as the Salvation Army hall. A cottage joined this and here the village shoemaker lived, by the name of George Pearce, him and his wife. She worked on the land. Now across the little roadway leading to the mill were two more cottages, rather lower down than the octagonal house which is there now. They had one large room downstairs and two small bedrooms. Mr Arthur Reeve and his wife Emma lived here. They had a son, Basil, living with them, and a daughter, Elsie, by his first wife. They were old and he had his hair in ringlets. He only had it cut once a year and the ringlets would hang right down to his shoulder and under a rusty old black hat. He was kind, and if we children met him he would say 'Hello old tuppenny'.

Next to them lived old John Lincoln and his wife Lottie. She was ill for many weeks and just lived on water. She had a bed downstairs. Anyone who came to the door, trades-people or whoever it was, could see all over the room and the bed. It was washroom, cookroom, bedroom. Everything was spotlessly clean there though. John was old and bent. He had to come to our back door for water for drinking, so while he was talking to my mother I would fill his pail and take it back home. Lottie was my father's aunt, a sister to his mother.

Then there was a separate house quite near the road. It looked quite large but it wasn't, because a big shed was under one of the bedrooms. When I was very young an old couple lived here by the name of Harris. The old lady used to wear a grey shawl, and May, the grand-daughter, lived with them. This old man was supposed to be very ill at one time and unable to eat, he was so sick. They sent for Canon Hunter at the Rectory and his daughter came to see what the trouble was. It was mid-day and the old man had just had his dinner taken up; hearing her on the stairs, for she had a loud voice, he whipped the plate under the bed. Most people had a valence round their bed at this time, so the dinner wouldn't be seen, but Miss Hunter was a dog lover and she didn't go anywhere without them. Presently one of them came out from under the bed with a chicken leg in its mouth. 'Oh, whatever have my dog found?', she said.

THE BLACKSMITH'S

Now across the road to the small house joining the blacksmith's. Here lived Mr and Mrs Rawling. He was known mostly as Billy Head. His mother lived with them, named Ruddy Seaman; I expect her name was Rhoda. Next to the blacksmith's shop lived Mr Albert Wade. He had three children, Elsie and Cecil and Dorothy. Now he wouldn't allow us in his yard to play with his children, but we did love to watch the sparks fly from his fire. Truly the village blacksmith did work under the spreading chestnut tree for there were two large ones here.

A brick and stone wall was near the very narrow road. This wall was tarred black and up above were the two trees and just behind, a very deep well. The roots of these trees were very thick and stood out of the ground, twisted and gnarled like small branches. Well I remember them! I had been up the blacksmith's yard, while he was out, with Elsie to see her pet mice. He came home unexpectedly, and he grumbled, and running down the yard to the road which was downhill I caught my toe in one and landed slap, bang, wallop in the middle of the road with the palms of my hands cut in several places. I didn't get any sympathy either when I got indoors. 'It was your own fault, you shouldn't have been there'.

Under the chestnut tree was a round, flat cement base for shoeing cart-wheels. How delighted we were to see these done, but we had to keep our distance. Zephaniah Jarvis was the carpenter who made the wheels. These were put on the cement base. The hub of the wheel was put into the hole in the middle. When not in use in summer time the blacksmith's girls and others like us would sit here with our feet in the hole.

Now the wheels. A strip of iron was cranked through a machine just outside the shop door, made into the exact size to fit the wood wheel. Then it had to be heated red hot all round. Now two men carried it with big iron tongs and put over the woodwork. Another followed with a can of water. Other baths of water stood handy, for as the hot metal touched the wood it began to blaze and the blacksmith would shout 'Water, water, water, water!' as he and Mr Jarvis hammered away, for it would catch fire in different places. The noise of the big hammers ringing on the metal made a lovely sound. Wheel-shoeing was one of our most exciting days.

TRADESPEOPLE

For several years this was my little world, except for my grandparents and aunt and uncle and cousins who lived up high above us at the end of the garden in a house which has been pulled down.

Into my small world came the tradespeople. I will put the usual ones first. Quite early in the day came the people with the milk. They carried a large can and into this they dipped pint or half pint measures. These were on handles which could be hung over the edge of the can. From these it was poured into the customers' jugs. The milk came from Hollycake Hall, brought round by the son, Alfred, or daughter, Lottie, in an upright pony-cart – the harness I remember was tied up with string.

The butcher came Tuesdays and Thursdays at this time, but before this the women had to walk as far as the bridges to the house which joined the common. Billy Milk was the butcher then and he lived there. Kingston's of Dereham, grocers, sent their goods round in a covered wagon. Orders were taken one week in advance, but before Christmas a Mr Harry Andrews used to bring round a hamper of lovely things to order. It made our eyes sparkle to see crackers and Christmas stockings and small boxes of crystallized fruit and quarter boxes of chocolates. We were allowed to sit up late so we could see the hamper – he always came quite late. An aunt used to buy Ella and me a small box of the fruit.

The fish-cart came on Tuesdays – just an ordinary horse and cart. Although herrings were fourteen or sixteen a shilling we still had only half of one at a meal. I have seen my mother take all the bones out of one herring which had been left and make it into a fish paste for us to put on our bread and butter. We had samphire in season. Now this was the cart where she bought her cods heads which I spoke of before. A village man came round with cockles and with mussels and winkles. I think he collected them from Dereham station.

The ironmonger came out from Dereham – he had a long dray cart – selling his tins, saucepans, china and paraffin which was in a tank at the back. He also sold firelighters. He would make tins to order, any size or any special ones that you liked to ask him. Every Friday a Mr Drewry called on his way from Dereham. I don't know where he lived but he brought the yeast round, in liquid form. One evening when he arrived it was windy, wet and dark. Mother said to him 'It's a very bad

Butcher Bone's shop and house.

night for you tonight' and his reply, 'Yes m'dear we always do get some sort of weather this time of year, don't we?'. This amused us kids.

Delivering the meat.

HAWKERS AND GYPSIES

Hawkers would come, some buying rabbit skins but only if the heads of the rabbits had been skinned as well. Others came collecting rags and bones. We saved all the shin bones which I have spoken of before. They would give us threepence for a sackful.

Gypsies came round selling saucepan lids, for the fire burnt out the lids very quickly and if they were not replaced the smoke got into the food. They sold paper flowers. Some were made from swedes and put on broom sticks – not the broom sticks we use but the ones which grow. Another would come with a hand-cart collecting jam jars and bottles. They didn't buy these but gave home-made windmills made of wallpaper and box-wood and wire. The scissor-grinder came round with his machine. It was a joy to watch him pedalling away and hear the sound of the knives on his wheel. Occasionally a man arrived with a barrel-organ with a little monkey perched on the top.

FLOOD AND FEVER

Now in August 1912 it rained and it rained for three days and nights continually. Corn was swept from the fields and quite a lot of damage was done. We had water rushing down the road past our house and the little road leading to the mill had deep holes made in it. For most of the time we children were in the bedroom watching things floating down the road past the house. There had always been a small amount of water running down here. This we called the Run. The meadows near the river were flooded and the road from the first bridge to the Lodge, and past, was completely flooded. Because of this we had a change in our food, for pike got out of the river into the ditches and couldn't get back, or didn't because we had them stuffed and baked.

Not long after I started school we all had scarlet fever and for almost all that summer we had to stay in the garden and we were not allowed back to school until the last ones had had it six weeks. Ben didn't get it at all. After this time an inspector came round to fumigate the house. This evidently caused a horrible smell and housewives dreaded it. He came and with a stick lifted the mat in the bedroom and said 'Oh, I won't use it, you're so clean my dear'.

THE METHODIST CHAPEL

Our father had been in the Salvation Army, he had been in the band. We didn't go to church but to the Methodist chapel. I have always been glad we were not sent to chapel but taken. At the time I first remember, the chapel building had not yet been completely paid for and so at each quarter of the year a Mr George Goward, who I presume was society steward, would get up and say 'It's time for the letting and the re-letting of the seats'. This meant that the members would pay so much into the building fund. My father paid for a seat and in all those years the family had used the same one. Mr Goward was a tall, lovable man with white hair and white beard. Before joining the chapel an old lady told me that he had been a very heavy drinker. If this is so he was a completely changed man.

On Sunday mornings we went to Sunday-school, then after lunch father took us to the afternoon service. Often we would have the preacher home for tea. In the evening we went to chapel as a family. After service in the summer we would all go for a walk. Winter evening after service we would have friends in and at one time a

Daisy's Chapel

friend of mother's, Susan Yarham, would read a book, a few chapters each week; or we would just sit and sing hymns. I wasn't always pleased to go to the afternoon service because my cousins, the Jarrett family, went long walks with their father, and I did love looking at the hedges and ditches.

PREACHERS

But going to chapel as a child had its compensations even then. One preacher was like a jack-in-the-box, for sometimes you saw him and sometimes you didn't. He was so enthusiastic about what he was preaching he would be all over the place, but he left his impression on me. He has a warm corner in my heart, although it's years since he died. These men would pray from their hearts and not from any paper or book and all older people were in tune with them, for suddenly one would hear a loud 'Halleluja' or 'Praise the Lord' or 'Yes Lord, do'. It didn't make sense to me then but I wish people would do the same today, for it would show they were interested in the prayer and not in toying with their own thoughts.

There was another preacher who had such a loud voice one could almost hear him in Dereham. We had an adult friend staying with us once on the day that he was preaching and she would giggle if anything amused her, so we kids told her that she would have to listen very carefully if she wanted to hear what he was saying. You can imagine what happened when he first opened his mouth! On another occasion a preacher came who my sister and I didn't like and we decided between us that we wouldn't ask him to tea – nor did anyone else. His home was at Shipdham. He came back for the evening service and for his text he took 'Brethren, have ye any meat?' We got into terrible trouble over this when our parents found out, for they had been out to tea themselves.

These preachers were good honest men believing what they preached and many, many times in later years, in times of trouble and nights of great pain, their words and texts have come back to me, giving me wonderful peace and comfort. These men walked miles to preach the Gospel, walking from as far as Reepham, and after taking two services would walk back in the evening.

On Thursday evenings we had a Band of Hope meeting. Here we were asked to sign the pledge never to drink strong drink. Many children in those days were deprived because of strong drink. I think at these meetings we each paid a few pence for an outing to Yarmouth. When the older people died these meetings ceased to take place.

THE SUNDAY SCHOOL TREAT

For the Sunday-school treat we had games on Mr George Rix's meadow at Woodgate. Unfortunately for us a relative fed his cows here so there were plenty of wet and dry pancakes and it wouldn't be long before you heard something like this:-

'Wha's the matter wi' that little ol' mawther, wha's she blarring for?'
'Oh, tha's narthin' the matter, she only now jammed into a cow's tad'.

Then someone would have to hunt for a thick tuft of grass or dock leaves to clean her shoes. After games and races we walked to the chapel for our tea which consisted of large slices of bread and butter or quarter slices of very thick bread and a piece of cheese. We would plead to have pieces of cheese with the bread and butter but we were forbidden and we couldn't just take a piece for it was brought round by the teachers. Following this we had plain cake and fruit cake, not anything else.

Methodist anniversary held in the Sandpit, Swanton Morley.

Some years later my mother sent some home-made jam to the treat. One of my brothers came home and said he'd had some lovely jam at chapel, why didn't she make some like it?

CHAPEL MEETINGS

We had happy times at chapel practising for services of songs. We once repeated one of these at a service at Billingford chapel. We had to walk there on a dark winter's night, and walk back. We always had a coffee supper after them. We held May meetings every year to commemorate the beginning of Methodism which was on May the 24th. On the nearest Wednesday to this we had a preaching service in the afternoon and then tea, at which a tea-table discussion took place on some subject arranged beforehand. One year there were so many people there this discussion went on until seven o'clock and the main service of the day was to take place at seven-thirty when about four ministers were planned to preach. These were lovely times, for we met people from all round the district. During the first world war Mrs Andrews of Hollycake Hall invited us to her house on Sunday evenings for hymn singing, because of the black-out.

We practised for the Sunday-school anniversary which was held every June outside in the school playground behind the village hall. The men teachers dug holes on Saturday evenings and erected a wooden platform and put white calico round, and on Sunday took the chapel organ down.

We had three services there. People came from all the surrounding villages for miles in horse and carts and later on, bicycles. I realize they didn't come to hear us but to meet their friends. Those interested drew near but those who wanted to talk stood around the railings two and three deep.

Also in the Sandpit, strike meeting, 1910, led by George Edwards, later Sir George, the founder of the Agricultural Workers' Union.

When I was older we held meetings on Monday evenings when five young men used to come out from Mattishall. Mrs Hilton and Mrs Beevis took it in turn to give them supper for they said these boys had to rush homework and couldn't have a proper tea. The kettle used to stand on a coal fire during the service. It was when I was eighteen years old that one of them preached on John 3:16. At that service my life was changed, for I had become lonely; my girl-friends were away or they had boy-friends and I was not particular interested in boys. I shall always remember the joy which came into my life and filled it. It has been with me ever since, a joy that no-one can understand except they experience it, and when I have been ill and alone for days, at times when waiting to have operations I had no fear, for I knew I had a God who was both friend and companion – someone I could always talk to.

THE SUNDAY SCHOOL OUTING

Now just about this time the superintendents of all the Sunday Schools in the districy amalgamated and a special Sunday School train went to Yarmouth from Dereham. We were taken in to Dereham by horse and waggon. I have mentioned before that all Sunday Schools went on a special train. We had to get to the waggons, which would take us into Dereham, by seven-thirty in the morning, for it would take some time for us to load up and get sorted out to make sure everyone was here. The nearest waggon to us was at Darby Yard at the bottom of Elsing Road. There were more to pick up here for it was nearer the village and almost everyone went, chapel or not. About forty of us got on the waggon once and when we reached the other one at Greengate some transferred from us to that. Boards were put from side-to-side for us to sit on. We met at seven-thirty but the train didn't leave Dereham until nine o'clock. My parents came later bringing the cripples, for they couldn't climb up into the waggon. We unloaded in The Fleece yard in Norwich Street, Dereham. We were there long before the train and what a hustle and bustle there was on the station. We watched for the first puff of smoke and what excitement when someone said 'Here she come, here she come round the corner!' and everyone surged forward to see the first of her.

Different compartments were reserved for different Sunday Schools and of course it was quite natural in the excitement to get into the wrong one, for a thing like this only happened once a year. We watched as the train passed windmills, for there were quite a lot on the marshes for draining them. We watched to see what the cattle were doing. If they were lying down we would be sure of a fine day, but if running around swishing their tails, it would be a stormy one. We arrived at about eleven or eleven-thirty at Southtown station.

At last we were there but we were a long way from the beach so, as we were always short of money, my mother and the cripples were put on the tram and the tin hat-box of food. Once mother forgot this and left it on the tram, but she had no bother to claim it for when she got to the terminal it had already been opened. I had to walk with my father. I do remember we walked through the Rows, these were streets just wide enough for a handcart to go through. There were many of them; they were mostly knocked down during the war. I also remember a round tower somewhere. The first thing we did was to go to Jackman's store on the beach to have some hot tea. We had threepence to spend as we liked and what a lot we could buy with it. Ice cream a halfpenny, sticks of rock a halfpenny, nougat and lots of other things. Then everyone went to the beach. Most of Swanton Morley went to

Setting off for the Sunday School outing to Yarmouth.

the same place; here they dug a large shallow hole and put coats and bags in it. It was for people to sit on too, that couldn't afford a chair. Baskets and bags and everything was left here, for they knew that some of the Beevis family would be here all day. I have a photograph of this somewhere. They were glad to leave their coats because people only had winter coats – there were no raincoats or light coats.

Once father had to take us two girls on his own, for some young lad had tried to give Fred a piggy-back and had dropped him and broken his leg. That summer a temporary shed was fixed next to the house with posts and sacking. Here Fred was put on fine days and had to remain until one of the men came home. This did mother and Ben out of their one day's outing so later in the year she took us on her own, by train. She took three cripples and myself. I don't know how we got to the station. We met some of father's sisters there; they also were having a day out so I went with my cousins. When I met the others again they had been given, on the pier where they were sitting, a half-pound bar of chocolate. Some lady had given them this, and it was marvellous for we had only had a halfpennyworth of anything before. On Saturdays my father used to give me twopence-halfpenny. I used to spend a halfpenny for Ben on sweets, a halfpenny for Ella and a halfpenny for myself. The other pennyworth of sweets was for the house.

WORK ON THE LAND

Sometime while I was still at school Mr D'Arcy died and his wife went back to America. A four-day sale took place at Bylaugh Hall – and my father was out of work. Our three boys were away in the army. The older cripple had his calling-up papers too. Claude was wounded. The other two were missing, one, Herbert, never to return.

My father had to work much harder now, harder than he had been used to, for he took a job on the land. The farmers only grew wheat, oats and barley, and root crops and kale for the cattle. These crops were sown in rotation. The root crops were pulled by hand and then the tops cut off by hand. They did two rows at a time across the field, throwing them into one row. Then they did two rows back, flinging them on top of the others so it made one row. Other men came with a horse and tumbril to cart them away. They were taken now to near the gate where someone else made them into a hale for winter use.

The cattle were fatted in the yards and buildings in winter. Mangels had to be put through a grinder which was turned by hand, chaff was mixed with them and fed to them by the bushel skipful by the cattle feeder. This is all the work he did in winter. The cattle were also fed bean meal and linseed cake. The cake came to the farm from the railway station. It was in slabs fifteen inches by two feet lengths and had to be broken by a hammer on a block. The cattle were given oat straw for night feeding. They were littered with straw every day but this was not disturbed until spring-time, then it had to be lifted by the forkful into tumbrils and the tumbril loads carted to a corner of a field and stacked. Here it remained for two years, after which it was put on the fields in heaps cromed down from tumbrils and someone had to walk about all day muck-spreading. There was no means of washing hands after doing this work before eating their meals. Pigs' muck was done in the same way and when the men came into the house the aroma seemed to increase!

Other heavy work was cleaning out the drains, ditches, dekes or dikes, whichever you like to call them; these had water in them most of the year. Trenches had to be dug by hand across the fields for land drains to be put in to drain the fields which were very wet. The men had to use their own tools for all these jobs, the farmer wouldn't find them. If it rained or snowed they couldn't leave their jobs, for if they did they wouldn't get paid their wages, and their wages were so small they couldn't afford to come home. They wore only leather boots, some also buskins and in summer, yorkers - leather straps below the knee to keep mice from getting up the trouser leg. They managed to keep themselves fairly dry by wearing a sack round themselves like a skirt held on by a strap, and another sack with one corner turned into the other for a hat and cape, tied on with string.

The hedges were always cut before harvest time so that the trimmings could be used for stack bottoms to keep the corn well above the ground. These bottoms were marked out ten yards by five yards and the corn was stacked heads inwards. All day long land workers had to walk. The ploughman with his team of horses walked up and down the fields, one foot in the furrrow and one foot on top. You could always tell a ploughman by his walk. My husband still walks the same way even today. The ploughing and drilling were done by the team-men. These men had to start work at five o'clock in the morning to feed their horses, get back home for their own breakfast and back to work at six-thirty in the winter. When there were several teams of horses on one farm no-one was allowed out of the stables until the head team-man was out, then the second and then the third. Going to the station or anywhere on the roads they had to go in this order. These were skilled men. Other men were allowed to use their horses for horse-hoeing between root crops, harrowing corn, rolling land, all walking jobs. The rollers were made of iron in three sections eight or twelve foot long. The men also had to walk all day hoeing and singling roots and although harvest time was great fun it was very hard work for all the family.

THE HARVEST

I can just remember the corn being cut by men swinging scythes, one behind another. I myself have counted thirteen men doing this at one time, the women workers going behind picking up the wheat or oats in armfuls and then taking a handful out would twist it expertly into a bond for tying the corn. More men came behind and taking two shocks at a time stood them up until there was a dozen or sixteen; these were put into orderly rows so that the waggon could pass between two rows and they would pitch them up from both sides to the loader on the top. A young boy would ride on one of the horses so that he would warn the man on the load when the waggon was going to be moved so that he wouldn't fall off. He would shout 'Hold yer', or 'Hold tight'.

I can remember being in a field at the corner of Park Farm Road and Elsing Road when the first sailers came into the field – I don't mean the little men in blue either – but the first sailer cutters for cutting corn, named so for its sails were like a windmill, turning the corn across the canvas where it was cut and dropped in rows. This was usually used for barley. Now it was women's work again to move one row forward onto the next and one row back, so that there were three rows now in one. It had to lay for several days to dry because barley fields were mostly laid down for next years hay. Seed would have already been sown earlier so the young green which had started to grow would be cut with the corn, and before carting it had to be really dry, like hay. If it was wet weather this corn had to be turned and turned again, perhaps day after day. My father and uncle were working here at the time the sailers were working. One said to the other 'What a wonderful machine it is, but it will do us out of work in the future.'

The self-binder was the next machine to come on the farm. It tied the sheaves with binder string ready for them to be stood up without the women's help. Both these machines had to be drawn by horses, two to pull a sailer and three to draw a binder, and they had to go at an even pace or the corn wouldn't cut. While the cutting was going on the old men, children and wives would gradually gather in the field to watch for the rabbits running. The rabbits themselves would go farther and farther into the still-standing corn and when nearly finished would make a bolt for it. People tried to catch as many as possible for these were the men's perks. After the field was finished the rabbits were laid out in rows. The head team-man doled them out. He had the first pick and his team-men followed, labourers next and the boys last.

Boys worked full days. There was the elevator boy. When the corn was carted his job was to see that the horse under the elevator worked properly. The horse had to walk round and round all day, only stopping when a waggon was emptied and the full loads put in its place. When the empty waggons went back from the stack sometimes we would clamber in and get a ride – it depended who was driving. In the bottom was a quantity of shelled-out corn and amongst it an amazing quantity of different insects. We didn't mind these at all. The elevator horse was attached to a rod so the elevator tines would take the sheaves to the top. The boy could stand or sit, it didn't matter so long as the horse kept at the same pace to get the sheaves up at the right time.

Other boys had horse rakes and they had a seat to ride on. The fields were raked several times and these boys would leave rows of straw and corn across the field. When the rake was full he had to lift a lever and the rake came up and left the rakings behind. These were collected and put on the top of the stack before it was thatched. As each stack was finished the thatcher came along. The stacks were works of art really, for they started small and gradually grew a bit larger as they went up and each part had to come out exactly even, otherwise they would have fallen over. The thatcher was very skilled. He always had a young man with him to damp down his straw and get his yelms ready and carry them up for him. Straw had to be pulled out from the heap by hand or fork, laid straight into a piece of stick. The yelms were about a yard wide. It took five yelms to make a sheaf. These had a stick at the top as well and string to the bottom stick. This straw was sodden wet and was carried up on the man's back to the thatcher at the top of the stack. The younger man, or mate, had to sharpen the brotches and carry these up the ladder. They were nut sticks, split, and were two-foot six inches long. Each thatcher had his own hall-mark, at the end of the stacks he made a little fancy shape.

These stacks stood all winter until the corn had time to mature and when no other work could be done. Then came the steam engine, the drum for knocking out the corn, and the straw pitcher, the water cart and the team of men for operating them. What a joy to hear the hum-hum of the engine as the straps whirled round, the beating of the drum feet as they worked up and down beating out the corn, the sacks being filled as they were hooked up to the drum, the smell of the engine smoke, but ooh! such a lot of muck and dust as the man filled sacks with chaff and colder – this was the short straw which was broken up.

At the time the oats were thrashed one always knew where a new baby would be born, for the father-to-be would ask the farmer for a sack of oat flights – the oat husks – for a baby's bed was made of these. Put into sheeting or ticking these husks made the bed. The parents didn't always have a cot to put the baby in either. If they had a chest of drawers then one of these would be emptied and the baby put in here, or a cot-shaped calico affair was made to slip over two chairs – two small ones put seat-to-seat – and the calico put over the chair-backs and the flight bed laid in.

Adult beds consisted of two straw palliasses, these were half-sized mattresses put onto an iron bedstead, mostly with a feather bed on top. Feathers were put into paper bags when a fowl was plucked. These were baked in the oven to kill germs. Then when they had collected enough the feathers would be stripped for pillows or beds. If you were well-off you had a horse-hair mattress or a flock one. The flock ones were like a rock garden – they were rather lumpy.

To get back to the harvest, girls had to work too. They had to take the dinners, and teas known as fourses. Most men had hot dinners taken to them, things like meat and onion dumplings or apple dumplings and they had vegetables in season, mostly runner beans and potatoes. These dumplings were mostly put into upright milk-cans – they were the shape of saucepans only deeper with a handle and a lid. These were easier to carry than a basket. Neither my brothers nor my father wanted their dinners taken. My brothers would say, 'Oh, we can earn our money without a girl helping.' I had to take my uncle's. At eleven o'clock I had to go indoors for a wash and have a clean pinafore put on, hair brushed and then I was sent round to Aunt Hannah. She sent her husband's dinner in a dish in a basket. It seemed a big basket to me, for I would only be about eleven or twelve at this time. I had to carry this with an arm through the handle, and in my other arm a bottle of tea, hot tea, wrapped up in a towel. I had to carry this up the Elsing Road as far as Castle Farm drift, and then to the fields beyond, sometimes down past the house itself. My uncle

A Fowler engine. The plate on the side shows it belonged to W.H.Riches of Swanton Morley. Kelly's directory of 1892 lists William Horace Riches as a farmer at Field House, Swanton Morley. The man leaning against the front wheel is Theophilus Barker.

never seemed pleased, nor did he smile, and I cannot remember ever having a penny from him. It was a long walk for a little girl alone – well I think so now, but I didn't mind then.

One day I made a mistake. I thought the men were in a field called Slodds and when I got there no one was in the field. I walked back and down the drift. The men were just going to start work and he hadn't had his dinner. I don't know if this is the day he left his dinner. One day I know he left two rabbit legs. On the way back I thought I would try the small one and it was so nice I ate them both. I have often wondered what he or his wife said at night-time. I've always had a guilty feeling about those two rabbit legs when I remember. It's only since I have been writing this that I realise why my uncle never smiled. He had lost his first wife early, his second one was an invalid with a bad heart who had to lay in bed downstairs for weeks in their one room. He himself had bad ulcerated legs. Huge they were, and open places on them. He had to work just as hard as the other men. He must often have been in misery, especially at harvest time when stubble would prick the legs and barley halms creep up his trousers. I have thought of him quite a bit since writing this.

The harvest wage when I can first remember was five pound for the whole harvest, however long it took. Sometimes it could be done in three weeks, I have known it to last seven. They worked all day till dark. If wet the men had to stay at home, for farmers wouldn't pay for days lost in harvest time. If the rain ceased during the day the steward would come round in his horse and cart and say, 'Come on boys, there's so many shocks blown down in this field and so many in that and they want setting up again.'

After the harvest was over perhaps the men would have a day or so off to do their own harvest on the allotments. They only grew barley on these allotments for the birds would eat wheat and oats if they were set in small plots. They used scythes to cut this. It would be carted into small stacks or even heaps and covered with all kinds of things to keep it dry. It would be carted to the allotments when most people had grown corn, for some grew root crops. This was so it would be easier for the engine and tackle to visit them.

Now this was a worrying time for the smallholders. Before the day for thrashing – or 'troshing' as they used to call it – sacks had to be found and sorted. If rats had gnawed them they had to be mended. This was done by button-holing round the hole with Phylls string and continuing with this stitch until the hole was filled. Special coal had to be ordered – huge lumps of steam coal. Often the engine would move at dusk and the sparks were as good as fireworks to us kids. Each allotment holder helped the other, or if he had more corn than the others he would hire an extra man. After thrashing, some of the rough corn was taken to the mill to be ground for pig food. The best corn had a sample taken out of it and this was taken to the Corn Hall in Dereham where little desks stood all about the floor. These had little metal basins on. Here men examined samples, smelling, biting and looking and then one was offered a price. The seller went from desk to desk to get the best price. My father once took me to the Corn Exchange in Norwich where the same thing happened.

He felt the loss of his eldest son very much, my father, and he was finding the work hard now, doing land work and missing the boys' help on the allotments, so I was asked to help him. I was still at school. I remember we had one field on our own. Here I weeded thistles in the corn, all on my own one day. It was a lovely sunny day and all was quiet except for the larks high up in the sky. I shall always remember that day because I loved being out in the middle of a field. I led the horse in the horse-hoe for him. I helped on the stack, taking the corn from my uncle on a tumbril to my father on the stack. He would take me on summer evenings down the by-roads to cut grass from the roadsides and bring home for animal feed. I used the wooden rake to collect any corn left on the ground and because it was war-time I went picking up acorns of which there was an abundance; and I went gleaning for ears of corn. My mother would persuade me to go out on winter evenings with him to help him feed the animals. Here I used to grind the mangel while he filled the skip and fed the animals. The cripples used to beg me to bring some strips of swede back and I expect one was put into the cutter on purpose and not by accident.

CHRISTMAS

Now I am coming up to Christmas-time. We didn't get much in presents. I had a doll's hat once, but I didn't have a doll. My sister had one, a big one, but it was kept in a box and only came out on birthdays, or holidays, or when one was ill. The Christmas dinner we had was a cockerel, fatted at home, and for the plum puddings we had large fat raisins, but these had to be stoned and as no-one liked this job they were brought out after tea and everyone had to help. Beside the raisins we had to help to chop the suet; this was bought in a large thick lump from the butcher's. Several puddings were made and boiled in the copper because the winter store of food was dwindling, such as apples and jam, so we had plum puddings for Sunday lunch several weeks instead of apple pie.

The D'Arcy family lived at Bylaugh Hall until 1917. Just before Christmas we had one nice outing to Bylaugh Hall where every year wives and children had tea in the servants' hall, that is, wives and children of the working men. We went at four o'clock, father driving us. The tables were spread with sandwiches and small cakes of all descriptions, the likes of which we had not seen. Afterwards crackers were thrown to us by the servants and footmen, boxes and boxes and boxes. Then each family was called by name and we were conducted by the head footman up the stairs to the billiard room where Mrs D'Arcy enquired about us. She gave each a bag of mixed nuts, a bag of sweets, an apple and an orange. These were all luxuries to us of course. Every mother was given a parcel to take home. One year when the parcel was opened there were two shawls for us girls in salmon-pink fine wool lace. How I loved these. We wore them over a coat of navy blue, the ends tied behind us. My father was given, as all outside staff were, a brace of pheasants, a piece of beef, a Christmas pudding, a Dundee cake and six mince pies. The farm worker was given at that time, if he was lucky, a brace of rabbits. Some didn't even get this. The only snag about this outing was, because my hair was always unruly and wilful I had to go to school with it in rag dodmans until three o'clock in the afternoon. I didn't like to go to school like this and I liked less to see the smiles on the teachers' faces as I passed them when I went in.

One Christmas it was very cold indeed. I remember my brothers going out handbell-ringing. It was bitter cold. My mother made a brown paper waistcoat for Claude and she sewed it on to him underneath his other clothes. They, the bellringers, were out all Christmas eve until midnight. They played outside our house and then came in for supper. Ella and I crept out of bed and watched them pass the bottom of the stairs. We saw our Christmas cake pass the bottom of the stairs as well. It was an iced one with jelly raspberries on top. There was quite a lot of noise downstairs as they thawed out, especially when Claude took his jacket off. 'Oh, you old so-and-so, we wondered why you never complained of cold'.

On Boxing day they used to go round again as far as Bylaugh Hall and Bylaugh Farms. When I was older I went carol singing with the chapel people, and when Ben and Ella had chairs they also went. Once it was so slippery that everybody fell down. We would start singing when suddenly one, or even two, would be missing and they would be laying at our feet. Even the wheel-chairs revolved several times. I think we were poor singers that year for there was such a lot of laughter.

I now remember how disappointed I was that we never had a Christmas tree. First we didn't have room for one and secondly we couldn't afford to trim one. Once Mum came out to the kitchen on Christmas day and asked 'What are you doing?'. I said 'I'm making Ben a Christmas tree in a pot'. I'd got one piece of holly in a little flower pot.

Once mother went to Dereham before Christmas. I couldn't have been very old. There was a white paper bag lying on the flour-bin when I went in. Ben, who was younger than me, was there. He looked at me and said 'Don't mob, don't mob' and so of course I looked, and Mum had bought one shiny decoration and this was in pieces. Ben had been there before me.

We usually had two or three friends in for Christmas tea, for ours was an open house where everyone was welcome. We had a little magic lantern in our house, we had it out at Christmas. It went with oil and didn't it smoke, but it caused quite a lot of fun each year.

The Dial.

VALENTINE'S DAY

The next event was on February the 14th, Valentine's day. This was made much of until recent years. All the neighbours took part. They would bring little presents and lay on the doorstep, one at a time, and then run away and hide. Once a big rag rug was put on our step, leaning on the door. It seemed to leap inside like a big black dog. Once we had a doily wrapped up in paper with a pig's tail poking through to represent flowers. Often a big piece of wood would be wrapped up to look like a ham, and as one went to pick it up it would be dragged away and if you went out to get it, it would go a little further. Mostly we had small things like crayons, books, pencils, but they gave immense pleasure.

PUBLIC HOUSES

There were five public houses in the village, the Horseshoes and the Plough have been pulled down, the Dial has been turned into a private house and the two others remain, the Papermakers' Arms and the Angel. There was another one, a partly fallen down one, called the Cherry Ground standing next to the Angel.

MORE VILLAGERS

Next to the church stood the Papermakers' Arms, kept by Mr and Mrs Sid Tye. At the far end of the row was the post office and shop kept by Mr and Mrs Mitchell, and next to it a cottage used for a warehouse which housed the paraffin tank and hardware goods. The pillar box was just outside the shop, in the wall which surrounded the rose garden where huge bushes and tulip trees hung. The Postmaster's son, Hooligan Mitchell, lived next to them.

The cottages next door to the Papermakers' Arms were very small. This is where Ted Porter lived. In the house next to the Papermakers' lived old James, who was a lovely old man. He welcomed all us children into his home and he'd stop and speak to us in the street, and all the smaller children would ask to take his hand and jump up and down. I have often been in his cottage. It had the usual sacks on the floor and one armchair in which he used to sit, one table and a chest of drawers, and one or two whitewood chairs. He was always happy. I can see him now, sitting near his window in a drugget jacket and trousers. We all used to call him old Jimmy Waddles but I think his name was Verdun. But it's the next house really I want to mention, for a pale woman lived here with a drawn face. She lived alone. No one seemed to know her or anything about her and no one hardly ever saw her except when she went to the shop, and so she was said to be a witch and us children would hurry past her gate. What a contrast to the man at the other end. One was shunned and the other sought after.

THE POST OFFICE

I think it's time to talk about the shop; the one near the church was the Post Office at this time. It was much as it is now, except you entered between the two front windows. The windows were decorated with pyramids of goods in boxes or packets, as were all shop windows everywhere, and beautiful and attractive they looked. The Post Office was at one end and there were two counters for grocery. It was like walking into Aladdin's cave, everything one wanted was there. If they hadn't got it you could have it in a day or two, for they would get it for you. The ceiling was completely covered with things which would hang, such as brushes, saucepans, spare lids, balls of string, rope. Anything which could be hung was hanging from the ceiling.

Just inside the door were sacks of sugar, peas, beans, nuts, rice etc. All these were weighed while you waited and were put into blue bags or newspaper. Butter and lard were in square blocks. This was cut and weighed as needed. There were two chairs in front of the counter, and behind it, facing the customers, were little tiny drawers, lots of them, for holding such things as pepper and cloves and spices which had to be weighed as well. On a shelf above were large green canisters which held tea and tobacco. These all had to be weighed as you waited for them. Below the drawers was a shelf with chocolate in halfpenny and penny bars and at Christmas time little sweet bird-cages were here, costing twopence, about an inch high.

The owners, Mr and Mrs Mitchell, had been master and matron of Gressenhall workhouse and brought out to live with them old Esther. Anyone having an ache or pain would go to her and and she would mix something up for them. She was a medium-sized woman always dressed in black, wearing a little bonnet on the back of her head. These were made of lace and ribbon and beads. She had one with deep purple ribbon on. Mr Mitchell was a thick-set man, always wearing a cap and glasses and a white apron. He was quite business-like. Besides selling the things I have mentioned they sold pork, killed on the premises, and paraffin and nails. When Mr Mitchell was ill and not expected to live the street from the Papermakers Arms was littered with straw to lessen the noise made by farm carts and wheel hurdles. The roads were made up of stone and the cart-wheels were iron so one can imagine the noise they made. This shop was closed during the first World War but for some time we were able to get goods if we went round to the back door.

The roads were made of stones. The farmers at one time kept them up; women

Town Street. Post Office and village store.

picked up stones from the land and they were carted onto the roads and then covered with marl, which was a white substance like clay. How I used to get wrong when the marl was first put on, for in wet weather it would stick to our boots. Even the Street and the main road into Dereham had grass growing on them. There were just three tracks where it did not grow made by the horses' feet and the cart wheels.

Later on I think the County Council took over the main roads and the District Council the by-roads. When this happened loads of stones were put on the road and a steamroller crushed them in. The roadman for Swanton Morley was Lee Harris, he worked alone. Each man did a certain part, they were called lengthmen. They had to trim the edges, open up the water gullies and fill up the holes in the roads. The by-road men had to break their own stones. Arthur Reeve, known as Little Arthur, would sit on a heap of stones all day, with a crome fork raking the stones and breaking them with a hammer. He always wore goggles.

Later on they had a boiler. This was for the main roads, where they heated tar. The road was swept and tar was poured on by the pailful and the dust swept back. After this they had a machine which could do larger stretches. Several men would do half the road, this was tarred and gravelled, and then the other side was done. In summer time this was dreadful for it would bubble up and come away from the road and boots and clothes would get covered with tar spots which wouldn't come out.

THE END OF SCHOOL DAYS

When I was thirteen years old the schoolmistress went round to my mother to ask if she would let me go as a servant to Hoe Hall as they wanted a young girl. I didn't go but kept at school till I was fourteen. One girl of my age did leave and went out to work. She had her hair pinned up on top of her head like they did in those days, and a fortnight later she was back at school with her hair down the back again, for if you

Town Street. The Papermakers' Arms in the foreground.

left your job you had to go back to school till you were fourteen. Service was the only work there was for girls to do, and every large house had a maid, even the schoolmaster, the baker and the builder had one. There were three at the rectory, three and a nanny at Hill House, three at Field House and a nanny, and at Waterfall Farm a skivvy, a little girl.

THE CLERGY

The rectory was a big place at that time with huge cement-paved kitchens. They kept two gardeners – a man and a young boy – and a coachman. The clergyman at this time was Canon Hunter, an elderly man who had a wife, a daughter and a son. The daughter lived at home, but the son only came home at certain times. They owned a boathouse and a boat by the river, which our boys used to use sometimes. To this clergyman every woman in the village had to curtsey and every man raise his hat. Boys and girls had to do this too. If the children didn't he would go round to the parents to know why they hadn't. Many a time one hid in someone else's back yard or hurried the other way when they saw him in the distance.

He was head of the village charities, so although we were poor we didn't get any charity because we were Methodists and did not go to his church. We did get two loaves of bread at Easter, for someone years before who owned Hill Farm had given one pound a year to buy bread for the poor at Easter. This supplied a great many loaves and this was taken to the village school and a list posted in the village of the names of the people who would receive them, the Parish Council distributing.

I haven't yet mentioned the doctor. The first one I knew was a Doctor Richardson and then a Doctor Howlett who eventually took over the practice. Doctor Howlett used to come round on a bicycle at first and then a motor-bike. He would take that in some most unlikely places, and then he had a car. There was no Health Service, everyone had to pay, so a doctor was never called unless it was really, really necessary. They would set bones and do all kinds of little operations, and everybody had to pay for what they had done – if they had the money. But there was a doctor's club. A person could join this by paying three-and-six a quarter. This was to cover the wife and children; the men paid into another club, or insurance, such as the Foresters etc. If any man went on the Club he was not allowed to be out after eight-thirty in the evening. It didn't matter if he was on the club for a hurt hand or even a finger, it was the order of the club that they weren't allowed out after eight-thirty.

Doctor Howlett was about when the Health Service was started. He said it was the best thing that had happened to him although he was dead against it at first. He found he was much better off because a great many of his patients had never been able to pay him and he couln't get his money, people were so poor. He said he himself had been really poor before it started. The doctors had to do everything for people, because no-one could get into hospital unless they were recommended by a subscriber to the hospital; and they didn't often have a doctor or a nurse to bring a baby into the world, for older women of the village did it on their own. It was the job of a very old lady who wore a cape and bonnet. Her name was Mrs Smith. She was called old Mrs Lapstone, she was never called Mrs Smith. The women also used to lay dead bodies out ready for the coffin. My mother have been known to do both these jobs. Late one afternoon she asked if I would go with her, for a Mrs Rix had died and it would be dark when she had finished laying this person out. I will never forget this, going to Mr Rix's house. The old man was sitting on the wash-bench outside the door. It was eveningtide and a lovely bright sun was setting which shone on his face. He had his hand over it and mother spoke to him. His reply was, 'The Lord giveth, the Lord taketh away. Blessed be the name of the Lord'. It was his second wife who had died.

LAYING OUT AND FUNERALS

When people died they were washed and clean nightdresses put on and stockings and padding and then laid on a board or a door taken from a shed. They were laid on this till the coffin came, which was made by a local carpenter. When they were in the coffin they remained in the house for about five days, the carpenter lending trestles to stand it on. A bowl of salt was placed on the body and a bath of salt water underneath. When there was only one room downstairs, and there were many houses like this, the family had to live in the same room as the coffin. The blinds had all to be drawn until the coffin left the house. I believe there were horse-drawn hearses but most people borrowed a horse and cart and the coffin was covered with a rug. Farmers were taken by horse and waggon. I knew a young man who shot himself and his coffin was not allowed in the church. His mother had his grave completely lined with flowers and greenery. These were pegged in with hairpins by Joe Canham, the sexton.

I was at school – I don't know how old I would be – when there was an epidemic of measles and a child died. Five small girls were asked to carry the coffin to the church. It was about three-quarters of a mile from the house to the church. Truly the child was small, but I think they forgot the coffin was oak. I, being one of the children, was frightened that I would let go of the sheet. I believe there were two sheets, one at each end of the coffin. I was one of the front girls and the fifth one carried a stool for us to rest the coffin on. The coffin was left open so that everyone could have a last look before going to the church and this child was the first time I had ever seen anyone dead. After a week or a fortnight another child died and the same four girls were asked to act as bearers, but this time we had to walk from Mill Street, by the river, to the church. When we got to the house we found a wheeled bier had been provided and we only had to walk beside it, which was better.

For normal funerals four bearers would be picked from the men of the village. To do this job they had to get time from work, rush home, change, go to the funeral then hurry home, change and go back to work. Lots of the villagers would go to a funeral, friends or no friends, for it was an hour out from the house and they would see someone different to talk to. It was really like an outing.

THE PENSION

I quite well remember old people getting the pension, for they were so excited about it. They got five shillings a week, I believe it was at seventy. I knew one by the name of James Brown who was due to take it the first week. How pleased he was. He had such a beaming, smiling face, but when he took his wages at the end of the week five shillings had been deducted from it by the farmer. The farmer told the foreman if the man was that age he wouldn't be able to do as much work. I remember it so well because of the bitterness of his workmates. The farmer owned the greater part of the village.

THE WORKHOUSE

Men kept at work till they dropped, for they had nothing except the Poor Law which gave them a bag of flour and two-and-six per week. If they became ill and could not work and look after themselves they were taken to the workhouse. Here, husbands and wives would be parted, only seeing each other for a short while on Sunday afternoons. My mother visited an old lady at Gressenhall. She found out then that old ladies were not allowed to wear nightdresses but only a short garment that looked like one. This was to save washing. My mother offered to wash this old lady's nightdress but she was not allowed. She was disgusted that old ladies getting out of bed had nothing to cover them below the waist. Several years later I visited my old landlady there on Sunday afternoons. She used to say every Sunday they had corned beef for dinner and mostly swedes with it, how she would like a beef pudding! One Sunday Mum made one for me to take, and I took it hot. While the nurse was away I fed her. When she came into the ward she said 'Smells as if someone has been cooking in here'. The old lady didn't take any harm from eating it for she wasn't ill, she was only helpless.

EDITH, THE SERVANT GIRL

Now I did want to mention Edith, the little girl who came to school with her hair tied with a bootlace. She always looked after my crippled sister at school, putting her coat on the hook and helping her on with it in the afternoon, because Ella would have to kneel on the dirty floor to have this done. When Edith was thirteen she was put out to service at the house next to the chapel. Then her family moved away to Bungay and left her there. She received sixpence a week. She had to live alone in a very small kitchen with no rug on the floor until she made a rag one for herself. She had to do all the rough work; her hands were like bursting sausages with chilblains. Although the house was only a few yards from the Post Office, Edith had to ask permission to post a letter and was told 'Yes, if you don't stop and speak to anyone'. When she wanted to go into Dereham to get new clothes she was only given such a short time to go and get back, that she ran the first length of a telegraph post and walked the next, all the way into Dereham and back again. She was allowed out each Sunday afternoon to the service at the chapel next door and then she had to go back to serve tea. She came to the evening service and stayed at our house after the service. On dark, winter nights she was afraid to go home so I had to go with her. I think I was only two years older.

A FRIGHT

There were no bungalows at Gooseberry Hill then, there were two tumbledown cottages, and near the road was a black, tarred barn. This was a dark road to travel – the banks were high and the hedges met above the road. One dark night coming back home a man walked out of that black barn behind me. How terrified I was, but I knew if I started to run I would have panicked and perhaps fallen, so I continued my usual pace. How glad I was to get home that night! I heard afterwards who the person was and he thought it was a huge joke to walk out there and frighten people.

TWO GIRLS

One of my cousins went to service at fourteen years of age to the Dereham station master. She used paraffin to light the fire one morning and she burnt herself to death. Another by the name of Lizzie – I won't mention her surname – was sent to service. My father took her and her box in the pony cart and left her, I think it was out Reepham way. Her mother came when my father got home to see if she had settled, but when she got back to her house Lizzie was there, for she had walked all the way behind the cart back home, and the next day my father had to go back and fetch her tin trunk.

LEAVING SCHOOL

Now it was my turn to leave school. I was fourteen in September, and how sad I was when the school bell went on Monday morning. I would have loved to have stayed on for I had missed much schooling because of ill health. I also hated changes and I still do hate them. I stayed at home until May, then my sister and I were apprenticed to a dressmaker in Dereham. I wanted to be a gardener, but I was laughed at. Girls couldn't be gardeners, what next would I think of? My next choice was to be a milliner, but 'No-one wants milliners these days', Mr Aldiss said. He said that the hats came straight from Luton and were already trimmed. So I had to be a dressmaker.

LODGINGS IN DEREHAM

We were taken to Dereham by pony and cart on Monday mornings and lodged at a small shop in Cowper Road. Miss Nelson kept this. It was only the front room of one of her cottages. She was a cripple too, she had a paralysed hand and arm and sladed her foot along. It was wonderful how she managed. She would take her good hand, open the other one with it and put knives etc. in it, or plates when she wanted to wash-up or peel potatoes. She lifted the arm up with her other hand and laid it on whatever she wanted to iron, and she managed. She didn't have much to sell – it was getting towards the end of the war. I believe Kingston's supplied her with stock. She only had just a few sweets, and locust beans were sold in their place; these were about the size of broad beans and looked like broad beans when they have turned black and seeded. Can't remember any beans being inside only a sweet substance. They were very nice. You ate the lot, the whole bean pod.

The war was still on but there were no ration cards. You got what you could. When we came out of Miss Nelson's door we could always see if there was an air raid in the district for little lights were under shades at every corner so that the whole street could just look and see this red light. If it was out there was a raid somewhere in the district.

To get back to Monday morning. Mother drove us to Dereham. She used to take a basket of food to last until the middle of the week. Anything else we wanted was bought by Miss Nelson and she was paid at the end of the week. We often exchanged food, for ours was home-made and what she had was bought. One night during the week my brother would bring us some more. He would drive his little pony, Tommy, and a friend came with him. Sometimes we would go to the pictures at the Memorial Hall. The friend who came with him had been christened 'Prince', for his surname was Wales.

APPRENTICED TO A DRESSMAKER

The place we worked was opposite the shop at Station Road corner. Miss Eastell was the dressmaker. We had to walk there each morning, my sister on her crutches, for they had no wheel chairs at this time. We worked from eight in the morning until eight at night, with one hour for lunch and half an hour for tea. For these hours we were paid one shilling per week for the first year and two shillings for the second year, but my sister was ill and she didn't finish her time. Once I had a terrible toothache, so one lunchtime I decided to go to the dentist and I had the tooth taken out. I was a bit late for work that day, in the afternoon. On Saturday when I was paid I only received nine pence instead of the shilling. This was always a sore point with me, for the lady hadn't thought of the pain I was in, nor had she remembered the times I had taken dresses home for her after eight o'clock at night in the summer-time. She did teach us well, though. Everything had to be perfectly correct. We learnt all aspects of the trade, but she said you will never finish learning because the fashion changes so often.

Our first jobs were putting press studs on to skirt plackets, and if ever you've tried these you'll know that they stretch because they were on the cross and it was so difficult to get them to lay level. Time after time they had to be taken off again and then put back. Another horrible job for us beginners was putting Russian braid round the hem of the older people's skirts. The skirts were nearly ground length and the braid with a little fringe on one edge was put on to save the hem wearing. Some were five-gored and some six, and they were very wide skirts.

There were hardly any paper patterns at that time. The skirts were cut out by measuring and laying a tape measure on the material. No pattern was used for skirts of any kind. Calico bodices were fitted on the customer and tacks were put in to mark the size that she needed. We worked all the week without bothering to pick up pins which were lost because this would have wasted time. And then on Saturday mornings all pieces were collected and all pins picked up. It would have been quite a lot of wasted time to pick them up as we went along. We also had to pick out the tacking cotton and use that again.

In summer-time, when there were thunderstorms Miss Eastell was scared stiff.

She would turn us out into the street, lock the door and run home to Bath Avenue. We had to go home as well, but we couldn't run – we couldn't get there so quickly and we often got wet. On snowy, frosty mornings it was dreadful for my sister to get to work. She would slip and fall often, because she had to walk on the road, she couldn't walk on the pavement. Time after time she fell and she couldn't get up unless I put my foot out so she could have something to steady her crutch against. I used to laugh, not because she had fallen down, but if I hadn't laughed I would have cried for her. People thought I was hard-hearted, one even said he would like to have taken a stick to me.

We left off work on Saturday noontime and mother would come for us in the pony cart. Even when we worked until eight in the evening mother supplied us with some sewing to do as well. We made tray-cloths with squared linen tea-towelling and we worked coloured spider webs into these squares. I sent one of these to a jumble sale only last year. When we were able we had to do blouses for ourselves. Mother never believed in wasting a minute and we had to show her the work when we got home to make sure we'd done some.

I have said the lady was a cripple. Well the toilet was quite a way from the back door. If she went in the dark, sure enough she would fall down. And if she did fall, sort of on to her back, she couldn't get up, so if she was away an extra long time I would go and look for her. I learnt, over the time I was there, how to get her up easily, that is if she didn't giggle which she mostly did, then we would be ages before we could manage it.

One time when I was cycling home a year or two later I saw an old man lying in the ditch. He stood opposite his gate on the other side of the road and he fell over backwards. I hauled him out. He told people afterwards he didn't know how a little thing like me could manage to haul him out, because he was rather wide, but I had had quite a lot of experience with Miss Nelson.

About three weeks before my two years was up as an apprentice a law was passed that young workers had to be paid nineteen-and-six a week. Now the extra money had to be passed on to the customer and work began to fall off. Some of us were not needed except when Miss Eastell had mourning orders or more work than she could do. She would then send for me for a week or a fortnight. From then on I worked at home, but it was difficult to get work done in a home like ours. When it was done I couldn't get my money, some people never intended paying either. No-one had money in those days. I shall always be grateful to Mrs Barclay of Hoe Hall. I had been making her some dresses and curtains and she asked if I could cover chairs. I said, 'Oh no!', but she said there's a chair in the servant's hall, would I like to try on it. To me it was not successful, but at the same time I was there a Norwich firm were doing chair covers for her in the drawing room, getting them ready for the seamstresses. So I got interested and when doing curtains in the front of the house I noticed how they were made, and when the men had gone home I went and examined them and from then on I did chair covers for some of the big houses in the district, and there I was sure of my money.

LEISURE TIME

There was not much to do in the village while I was at school. I had heard of whist drives but I didn't know what these were, except the school would be dirty in the morning with matches on the floor and it smelt dreadful. On Sunday mornings the men used to meet at Sophia Jarrett's wall, opposite the garage, to relate all their news and to hear all the gossip of the week. Sunday evenings they would take walks round the roadways then across the footpaths to see if Old John, or Old Tom had ploughed a straight furrow, because the fields looked beautiful with their straight furrows then. Or they went to see if somebody else's garden was better than theirs, or else they would lean over somebody's pigsty just to discuss these, just for something different to do. One place we were advised not to go to on Sunday mornings was Pennyspot bridge, for gambling was illegal in those days and the men would get out of the village and play pitch-ha'pence there. On Sunday afternoons the whole village, mostly, would take a walk down Mill Street. If you wanted to hear the village news or see what people were wearing this was the place to go. My parents never went there, they went to services instead.

Daisy's grandparents at Mileham, Ben and Caroline Nichols with a neighbour between them. Ben was coachman at Mileham Hall.

A similar walk took place in other places on Sundays. We went to Mileham one Sunday to see our grandparents, Ben and Caroline Nichols. Somewhere by the side of the road lay a huge drain waiting to be put under ground. The pony shied and mother was pitched into a ditch on the other side of the road. Her arm was painful and during the day it became more so and more swollen. So coming home in the evening my father decided to go round by Dereham and call on the doctor. Quebec Road was full of people walking and when in Dereham later Mum asked what had been taking place the shop assistant said that was the usual place to take a walk on Sundays.

A MISFORTUNE AND A MISADVENTURE

When I was working in Dereham an awful thing happened to my father. He was taken to court. It was like this. He had asked the farmer he worked for for a bag of chaff and was told he could have one. At leaving-off time the man he worked with said to him, 'You go home Alfred, I'll fill you a sack of chaff, and take it across to your allotment'. The allotment had one of the furze huts on it, with an open front.

The bag of chaff was put in here and stood there for four days. When father was working there with the horse and cart he brought the sack home. Half way the policeman stopped him and asked if he could look in the sack, and to father's horror it was like Benjamin's sack – the old man had put some corn in it as well, on top of the chaff. My father couldn't do anything about this for he was in posession and he couldn't tell who put it there. He was taken to court and fined six shillings. Billy, the old man who'd put it in, was a peculiar little man, and his speech was not quite correct. But father couldn't blame him because he would perhaps have been put out of work.

Billy used to visit The Angel quite a lot – most evenings in fact – and on his way home he would collect the eggs from his hen-house. The particular night I am thinking of was a very windy one. He went in to get his eggs and a gust of wind blew the door shut with a bang. This jarred the twist button which fastened the house and Billy was secure for the night! Next morning when the men were going to work they heard him shouting, 'Let me out, let me out'. He had got his head down by the pop-hole where the chickens come out. The twist buttons were only shaped pieces put on the post loosely with a screw.

WINTER

The winters were terrible in our schooldays with snow and ice and frost. I have seen icicles hanging from the shed roof almost to the ground, as thick as my wrist at the top. One winter the jug of water in our bedroom was frozen solid, and when it began to thaw the jug burst. And that night even the urine was frozen, under the bed. To keep ouselves warm we used stone hot water bottles. I believe they were beer bottles actually for they had handles on them; a round one and a flat oval one. We also had bricks, heated in the fire and wrapped in flannel, put into our beds when it was very cold.

If any of us had earache in the night a piece of tile, like the tiles which were on the house roof, was heated and wrapped and we laid our face onto it. If we had toothache we had a cabbage leaf, wiped and warmed, and this was tied with a handkerchief round our heads. I remember father getting up one night from his bed to go out into the garden and gather a leaf.

One winter night we were huddled round the fire in the big room with our winter coats on. A linen horse was at our backs, covered with coats and rugs. It was a dreadful night. Sacks were nailed up outside the back door so the wind blew them to the door, covering up cracks and the keyhole, and still we were dreadfully cold. I heard in the morning that the shepherd's hut had been blown down a hill somewhere with him inside it, but I wasn't old enough to understand. Often in the evenings we couldn't get near the fire because the working men's clothes were there. These had to be dried for the morning, and the leather boots, for there were no water boots. The coats were mostly thick blue disused railway coats. Oh, they were thick and heavy and took a lot of drying.

We didn't have very big fires either. Most fireplaces had a false bottom in to save the coal. This was an iron frame, just like the ordinary bottom, on four feet about an inch high. We had extra good fires when large hedges of thorn were cut down. If the men stopped after time or during their mid-day break to trim them they were entitled to have the thorn bulls. These were most awkward pieces and often were put on the fire across both hobs and allowed to burn through in the middle.

The false bottom was a lovely place to roast chestnuts. We had some each year because father worked on the park, but the keepers were not very pleased if they knew someone had picked them up because they were food for the pheasants.

I have said the winters were very bad but the roads were cleared quite reasonably. Every man would take his spade. He wouldn't be asked, he'd just look out of the door and see other people doing it and he would go too, every man. And farmers kept snow-ploughs handy. These were just two long boards fixed like a 'V'. They had an iron toe where the boards met at the front and they were drawn by horses. The horses' shoes were roughed at the blacksmith's shop. Instead of ordinary nails they had sharp, pointed ones which stabbed the frozen roads. When the snow was very deep the farmers would send their men to dig out the roads. One year the snow was so deep that sheep had to be dug out. These could only be found by a small brown spot in the snow. It was so cold one day, I remember carrying a milk can when it rained and as it rained it froze on the hedges in little icicles, and around my face and scarf. To get about the slippery roads we wore men's old socks pulled over our boots. It helped to save us slipping and also helped to keep the wet from getting through our leather boots.

THE SHEPHERD

I have not mentioned the shepherd yet, have I? His was a hard life. Most farmers in those days kept sheep, if only a half-dozen. At lambing time the farmer would have the lambing yard made well away from the village across the fields. The shepherd was provided with a hut which had a bench for a table and another place to lay down. Then he could snatch a little sleep, for he would be away from home for three weeks or more. He never went home during this time except perhaps to change his linen. But the family would take his food and sit with him afternoons or evenings. Other people were discouraged from going for fear of frightening the ewes. Even when his people were there he had to go out and leave them, for perhaps one of the sheep would be needing his help.

The fold was made up of iron hurdles on small iron wheels but the lambing end was made was made of wooden lifts, these were wooden hurdles. Wheat straw was yelmed out to six-foot lengths and tied to the lifts and fastened there by liggers, these were poles about twelve feet long and used lengthwise to hold the straw bunches in place. They made straw pens at this end of the fold to hold just one sheep, like little houses. This was for the sheep while it was having its lamb.

The shepherd didn't have to go out to get his sheep in, for when they were due for lambing they would come of their own accord. The sheep at other times would be penned out on fields of swedes or kale or grass. First the sheep would eat the tops of the swede and then a man was sent to dig the root out for them.

Oh, the noise these wheeled hurdles made, nearly as good as some of the singers of today! They screeched and squeaked as they moved. This reminded me of the noise that the yellow-hammers used to make, for there was a huge flock of them, especially just before one got into Dereham. Hobbies had a wood-yard there on a small field and these birds seemed to love being there. They were in flocks and flocks and they made an unbelievable noise. It was lovely to go through there and see them flying round. To move the hurdles a horse was hung on to about a dozen and then when their new pen was ready the shepherd and his dog would take the sheep, perhaps with the help of a boy. They would fill the whole road.

DROVING

All animals had to walk, many cattle walking miles going from this district to Norwich market. I was talking to someone only in 1979 who was a farmer's son, and he used to drove cattle from Mattishall to Norwich and just before he got to Norwich he would put them into a loke at Costessey and then have a little sleep himself and give the animals a rest before going into Norwich. There were special drovers who did nothing else except drove cattle, and everybody had to have gates on their gardens and fields, if not it was more difficult to keep the animals together. When on the road they would get frightened and if a gate was open or a hole was in the hedge they would make a dive for it and others would follow. Miles and miles these drovers would walk. Anybody could hire them, it was their job.

TOWN MEADOW

A big herd of cows was kept at Castle Farm. They used to be on the Town Meadow and a bull was kept with them. At five o'clock every evening one would see the milk float coming up the Meadow to catch the night train at North Elmham. In the summer time when we saw it we would dash off home for we knew it was tea-time. On Sundays someone else drove it and would go by a different route. It would come up through the Drove, a place by the side of the river, into The Meadow and then cross over at the ford which was at the bottom and follow the river on the other side and come out where the doors are on the other side of the second bridge. There were no doors there then and one could walk here. I always believed that it was the old road from the village. I noticed the doors had been put on and enquired of my father and he said, 'You mustn't go on that ground now'. The driver who came this way would follow the river to Worthing. The week-day driver would go up by the rectory and along the road which now goes through the aerodrome and down by Worthing church.

We used to play in this meadow by the church and down by the river end there were parts of houses and groundsels of others. We played amongst them and would take our boots and stockings off and cross the ford. By the hedge there was a great patch of blue violets. Many is the time I have gathered them. The Castle Farm ladies used to come to church up this meadow and over the stile at the corner of the churchyard. At violet time I would go round the churchyard and over this stile to my special patch of violets. They were beautiful. The parts of the houses we played amongst was the place where the old village had been before the plague.

The Castle Farm was so named because there had been, years before, a castle on an island in the river near here. I think my father said he remembered Castle Farm being built. Anyway, this is what he said about it: it was going to be built on the Elsing Road but it would have been in view of the windows of Bylaugh Hall and so it had to be built in a hollow so that they couldn't see it, for the family by the name of Lombe, owned the whole village.

THE WHITE HOUSE

Another place we used to go to was the White House down Mill Street with the pond in front. A family by the name of Yarham lived here. There were several children around my age. One mealtime I was asked where I had been and I told my parents I had been to the Yarham's. I said, 'There's a lot of trenches at the back of their house and they're full of water'. My father answered, 'Yes, there would be, for there was an iron-foundry there once'. Just inside the gate was, and still is, a domed well. I was told that pilgrims to Walsingham used to call there for a drink.

At that time there was also a paper mill, or part of it, standing at the side of the waterfall, but it has long since gone, as is the house which was on the corner before turning for the bridges. This was a thatched one and was burnt down in my time. We used to run in and out of the part that was left.

HIDDEN TREASURE

I have mentioned earlier that I lived mostly amongst older people. We used to hear them talking about the hidden treasure. This had been hidden in a pit, for pits were always full of water in my childhood. They said – my grandparents, Mrs Golding and Mrs Spelman, all very old people – that there was trouble in the Country. I should imagine it was during Cromwell's time. We heard them saying that the chest of treasure was put into a pit but when the trouble was over and they tried to retrieve it the handle came away with the rope. We children used to peer into the pit when out blackberrying, for my father had pointed it out to me. We went that way one day by pony and cart and as we were going along Father flicked the whip and said, 'That's the pit with the hidden treasure in'. At the present time it belongs to Mrs Keith. I have thought a lot about it lately and surely, if it was a big chest, more than one person would have to know about it and perhaps one of them rescued it and put the rope and handle back. I believe the silver had something to do with Hoe church, because it was supposed to be Hoe church door handle which was on this chest. It would be fun if at some time it was found. I wish I had asked more questions about it.

AURORA BOREALIS, THE CIRCUS AND ZEPPELINS

One night our mother woke us up to see the aurora borealis, for she said it was something we might never see again in our lifetime. It was just before the first world war. I did see it again after I was married, just before the second world war. Then the whole sky, right across, was a glowing rose colour all over, a most marvellous sight, far better than the first time I saw it.

Another time she disturbed our sleep was very early in the morning when the circus people were moving from Reepham into Dereham. We saw the elephants walking and other animals, small dogs and ponies. How our mother knew they would come so early I don't know, but she didn't want us to miss anything. After this time we only used to see the caravans, horse-drawn ones, for the caravan people used to use Miller's Lane instead of coming up the big hill near the church. Always before Dereham fair we had a mini-fair in Swanton Morley. A few caravans would stay on the village green and have stalls like shooting, darts and a small roundabout. We used to get used to the caravan people and we'd play with their children.

They used acetylene flare-lamps at that time. The place was all lit up the night Dereham was bombed. The officers at Bylaugh had a party on too and they had lights all over the place. Suddenly the police and soldiers came. The fair lights were put out suddenly and we were advised to get home as soon as possible. I ran up from the sandpit, over the top and down to our house. By this time there had been several explosions. Just as I got into the yard my mother and Herbert came out of the house and we looked up to the night sky. The zeppelin was as clear as daylight and it wasn't long before we heard other bombs.

Soldiers were stationed at all farm buildings in the village. That evening my father had let a soldier have the pony and cart to get his wife from the station. They had got some way on the road near the bungalows which are there now. At that time two stone cottages were in the same place. Just this side of them on the opposite side of the road there's an ash tree. The soldier, hearing bombs, put the light out and got under the tree when suddenly bombs dropped behind him in the field, almost opposite the cottages. I should imagine they saw the cart lights moving and that is what they aimed for. There was a tremendous hole in the field and the cottages were cracked right down the side.

Later we heard bombs drop in Dereham. I had an uncle living in Dereham at that time, he was in Church Street and he said that he had to crawl home over dead bodies. Many people afterwards went into Dereham to see the damage which had been done, and dust was on everything. I remember going to the garden where Allwood's, solicitors, are today and there was a big bush of huge redcurrants but they were absolutely grey, covered with dust. I don't think so very much damage was done except to Cave's shop, which was the photographers in Church Street, but four people were killed. I had the cutting from the paper until a few years ago when I lent it to someone and I never had it returned to me. I wish I still had it today.

JOE CANHAM

I have mentioned the handbell-ringers before. Well I must bring to life the man who taught these boys to ring, old Joe Canham, old was an endearing term really. Old Joe Canham, he was sexton at the church and his wife, a very small quiet woman, was the church cleaner. they had five daughters, all older than myself. Then suddenly from nowhere came a son, named Alex. I believe he belonged to Mr Canham's sister. When one of the daughters was getting married and the Nosey Parker of the village asked Mrs Canham which one, she said 'Oh, my daughter Josephine'. Apparently all had Josephine as a second name!

But it was her husband I wish to remember now. They lived next to the butcher's shop not far from the present Post Office. He was a gardener for Joseph Springall, the builder, who lived at Greengate House. While Joe was there he made a replica of Swanton Morley church. It was the wonder of everyone who passed. It stood on a mound of purple aubretia and was in the garden until the Springall family died and then it was sold. Joe did wonderful things and the teen-age youths loved him for he taught them to ring the handbells. He put ships in bottles. He made a policeman which looked like life and when one stepped on a certain place on his path this policeman came to meet you. After a time he had to restrict this for people were afraid to go round to his house. They must have had a guilty conscience. When I went to the door the policeman sat quite harmless on a bench near the back door.

Joe was the first person to have a gramophone, one with a large horn, and he would play it in the summertime in the garden to the wonder of all around. He was the first person to have a cat's whisker wireless. He made it himself, and many other things. That's why the young men liked to go round to his house. Later in his life he bought land, two old cottages and their gardens, and built his own bungalow, the first one to be built at Gooseberry Hill. He was not just satisfied with building it, he had carved woodwork everywhere, oak posts with different heads and faces to

Joe Canham's carved porch.
Lord Kitchener.

Joe Canham.

support his fence. Some of these can still be seen at the bungalow near The Angel. I'm not sure if there are any left at the original bungalow. He made a fountain that worked, and once he whitewashed the lower part of his greenhouse and marked it out like curtain net with tassels on. He and his wife were great workers in the church. He rang the bells, he also dug the graves. Today they cannot bury in Swanton Morley churchyard because the graves cave in. It did in those days as well, but Joe knew the way. He made a frame the size of a grave and as he dug a foot or so he would fix a plank in it at the top, like they used to brick wells. The well-sinkers made their wells from the top and dropped them as they went along. For all his cleverness Joe was a most unassuming man, small, wearing glasses and a cap. He was very well loved. Canon Hunter died and I suppose Joe dug the grave. I believe this one was lined with flowers.

THE REVEREND BARRY'S FAMILY

The Reverend Barry came in Canon Hunter's place. He had two grown-up daughters and two younger sons. I believe Mrs Barry was his second wife. They were a good family. He visited every one of his parishioners once every year and always when they were sick or in trouble he was there to help and comfort. He visited us several times when he heard about my brothers being wounded and killed. I don't think he was a very strong man, for once a month he had a day in bed and his wife would not let anything or anyone disturb him. If anyone was ill a milk pudding was sent from the rectory kitchen.

The oldest daughter worked on a farm during the first war and was a friend of the farmer and his wife. The next daughter was a very sick person and almost blind. How she came to visit my mother I don't know, but she came each week to ask if she would make her a cake of some kind. She used to show mother the sores she had on her hands and arms, poor dear. Once she said she wanted the cakes to eat in her bedroom and we thought perhaps her stepmother was rather tight on housekeeping. For a time we didn't see her and then we heard that she had died. The Reverend Barry, her father, came later and thanked mother, but never told her what the daughter's illness had been, but I think later mother realized that she had been helping a diabetic to get things she should never have had. My mother had been a cook in her single days and many people came and asked her to make cakes, so she didn't suspect this young lady at all. Mother won many prizes for her bread and cakes at the local flower shows which were held at Swanton Morley House.

CELEBRATIONS

When I was about eight years old it was the coronation of King George and Queen Mary. For this, every person in the village who wanted to, sat down to a meal in the open air. Trestles and tables were set up in the Town Meadow – the meadow in front of the church. The older people always seemed to be able to arrange things more easily than they do today, for when the present Queen's coronation came, they had one person to cook the meat and arrange the food, and there was not enough to go round. The committee arranged sports and shows for everyone in the village; old-age pensioners were given tea and biscuits, but Ella and Ben, the two cripples, were never given a penny or invited to the show for pensioners. I was too proud to draw the attention of the committee to this. But let's go back to King George's coronation. All the households near The Street did the cooking. The meat consisted of huge joints of salt beef and roast beef. These were carved at the table. The salt beef was cooked in the poor people's coppers, the roast beef was cooked at the mill bakehouse. Other people cooked plum puddings in their coppers. I can remember sitting at the table with my mother and Mrs Golding. Races took place along the Street from the Dial to the shop as they used to do at Whitsun. This was the time when members of some club or other, Foresters or Rechabites, had a dinner at the Dial clubroom. It was known as the Club Feast.

Sports took place along the Street at the same time. The men didn't have a half day then, so they got up early in the morning and prepared for it. There was a good team spirit in the village at that time. I know they got up early in the morning before going to work to prepare for it, for I remember them talking about the snow. One Whit Sunday, as father went to bed, he said 'Try and wake me at three in the morning so I can go and help to set up the stalls', and joking he said, 'If there's deep snow you needn't bother'. At three o'clock Mum opened the curtains and said to him, 'It's three o'clock, but you don't need to get up for there is six inches of snow'. Naturally he didn't believe her and had to get out and look for himself. I believe these sports were thought a lot of. I used to hear the old people talk of stalls each side of the street. They talked of the winkle and nut stalls, they didn't have them in bags, they were sold by the mugful and tipped into their pockets and they ate them as they walked about. I think the last stalls were set up at the beginning of the First World War.

DEMON DRINK

My brothers all being older than I, except Ben, used to bring home tales of the happenings in the village and we heard their news at mealtimes, for we all had to be home and round the table for every meal, and on time.

There were plenty of people who would drink in those days. There was a Watkins who lived on Greengate Hill. When my father had been to Dereham late to fetch someone from the station he would have to watch out for him and get out of the cart and perhaps lay him on the side of the road. Another person of this type was Ted Porter. I saw him one day coming home from the Royal Norfolk Show. That day he had blood all round his neck. There were two other men in the village with large families who really liked their drink. The men had Saturday afternoon off after the wartime, a cricket club was formed and these two would go out on Saturdays and often didn't get home again until after Sunday tea-time. I heard the boys talk of one man who liked his drink. He tied his donkey cart to a field gate and when he went to the pub they took it out and put the donkey in the field, put the cart shafts through the gate and harnessed the donkey to it again. I also remember hearing of one man who fell out of his cart at Claypit Hill, Elsing Road, and killed himself.

ERRANDS

I did mention one of my errands on Saturdays was to buy apples. When they first came I used to go for threepennyworth at the house called High View. Farmer Harrold lived there. The servant would cross the road and pick up the windfalls from the orchard, but they didn't sell gathered ones, so for these I had to go to Woodgate, to Easter's farm, the one with the barn on the corner where the road sign says 'No Road'. I should think it would be about a mile away from our home. My cousins would sometimes go with me. They didn't go each week, but I did because these apples were hard and green and would store well. I would get a stone for sixpence. It was a lot for me to carry. We took pillow-slips to put them in until my sister had worn the top of her dress up, then the skirt was made into a bag with a draw string and was kept for getting apples. We would sling the bag on our shoulder and carry them on our backs for a short way and then have a rest, and then carry them in our arms alternately, with rests between for us to eat the apples which had been put into our pockets for the purpose.

MY FAIRY HOUSE

It was by going for the apples I saw my fairy house. It was just before we reached the farm. Standing endways to the road it was a long, whitewashed, low, crooked house, thatched to just above the doors and windows. The bedroom windows were in the roof. All the windows had small diamond-shaped panes. The front door opened outwards, so if you stood the wrong side of it you would get knocked over. An old couple by the name of Peek lived here. They kept a lot of goats and no-one liked him visiting them in the evenings, especially when he went into a warm room, he used to pong of goats. I think they were retired gentry. I was privileged to go in one day and I was very much amazed to see a huge oak beam, not at the roof but standing up in the centre of the room. When I was tiny, having arrived on my father's shoulder, a Mr Russell lived here. His daughter was Maggie Russell, our schoolteacher. Later it was sold and a young man pulled it down and built a modern bungalow, standing in the opposite direction. I felt it was a great shame for this to be destroyed for it was a building of great beauty. Several huge cherry trees stood near and around the house and a large black dog came to meet you at the gate.

SOME HOUSES AND PEOPLE

Before one came to the fairy house there was a farm. Here lived a Mr Pye. I don't know if he did any work, but he was always dressed up as a gentleman and he went to church every Sunday. I never saw his wife. When people told him anything he would say 'Oh my!' so of course he was always talked about as 'Oh my! Mr Pye'.

On the road just past the Peek's house, the fairy house, was the Horseshoes public house. Here lived a Mr and Mrs Trollop. He had a forge here, by the side of the pub, where he shoed horses and did the repair work. His wife took in washing and this is where the square stove was in the middle of the room. The front of this house was level with the road. You went into the room at ground level, but when you went round to the back and the door was opened, inside were five or six steps and you looked down into the living room to peoples' heads, so when the door was open you could see all over the room. The shoemaker's house in Town Street was like this, on level ground at the front and several steps down inside the house to the living room floor.

There was another house I would like to describe but I just don't know how. The three houses in fact have all been pulled down. I want to describe the one my grandmother lived in. She was like the old lady who lived in a shoe and had so many children she didn't know what to do, for she had sixteen who all lived to adult life. It was on the high ground at the back of our garden, and yet part of it was on the road. Strangers used to stare at it. It was at Gooseberry Hill. The yard leading to it is still there, with the brick and stone wall. It had one room on the ground side and a small yard surrounded with a brick wall and gate. But the main house was up on the hill. I only remember this room on the ground level being used to store potatoes and tools, but the staircase led up here, although it wasn't used then; one had to walk up the hill, past the stone wall to the back door. But we will go up this staircase in imagination and we shall find ourselves on a small square landing after the trap door is closed, so facing south you would see a small closed-in pantry; behind you would be the front door; on your left you would go down two steps to the living room. This was above the room which was on the roadway, but turning to the right one went up five or six steps and would find yourself in the kitchen with the oven, the fireplace and a shut-in cupboard in which was the copper. On the opposite wall the staircase led upstairs, but underneath it was another door which led to a room used as a bedroom and called the by-hole. We're now right at the top of the yard so this house actually was on four levels, the ground floor, the living room floor, the landing and the kitchen. It must have been very tiring to live there. The front door was never used except for funerals.

A huge elm tree stood at the end of the house and they were always frightened to go to bed in the gales. There was a shed nearly opposite the back door and here all the home-made beer was stored. I wasn't allowed in here, but I do remember seeing the barrels and bottles. The house had two staircases to the bedrooms, but they couldn't go from bedroom to bedroom unless they came downstairs and went right through the house. The bedroom windows were in the roof.

Another place which might be of interest was Park Farm house. All my childhood people believed the house was haunted. The family of Mr Roy Money lived there and the children came to school, but they were never interested to know anything about it except there was a locked door. When it was opened many years later an old man by the name of Jimmy Pearce said all it contained was an empty wooden box which had a hole right through it. There was also supposed to be a headless horse-rider seen at times riding across the fields at Park Farm, and farther down the road at Pennyspot a coach and horses were heard often at night coming down the narrow back drive which leads from Elsing Hall. A daughter from there was supposed to have eloped and this was the coach she used at night.

THE END OF THE WAR

While I was still working in Dereham there was an epidemic of 'flu, a rather bad kind, in October 1918, when whole families had it. We all had it at home and were lying around everywhere. I went back to work in Dereham and when I got there I had such a terrible pain in my head that mother went with me to the doctor who said I needed another week at home. While waiting for her to do the shopping the news came through to say that armistice had been signed and by this time Dereham market was crowded. I was in the market and someone reported me being there to Miss Eastell, so when I did go back to work I was in trouble, for she said if I was well enough to stand around the market I was well enough to go to work.

After this my brothers came home and almost the first thing Claude did was to go to Dereham to Holman's shop and buy me a bicycle. I had by this time learned to ride on a friend's bike, for there was a family in Dereham who had been most kind to me and my sister, a Mr and Mrs Eglen and their daughters Violet, Alma and May. They had taken us to their home in the little time we had to spare in the evenings, and summer times we had taken their bikes out and they had helped me. I wish I had shown more appreciation to their mother, but young people only think when it is too late. I was very happy with this bicycle, for my friends had gone to service away from the village or they had found boy-friends, and my sister could not go walks with me. I loved going rides on my own. I noticed more of the fields and hedgerows then.

BILLY AND CLAUDE

Billy was home from the army now, but there was no work for my brothers. Younger men had grown up while they were away and were doing their jobs.

Claude went to work for a week or two with a neighbour's nephew, Harry Dawson, who was working away from home on steam engines, but Claude did not like the grease and dirt and smoke and so eventually he got back to land work on the farm he had worked on before going away and he continued there until he died. He was the brother who was wounded in the back of the head and he died from an abcess on the brain, yet got no army pension.

Billy was worse off. He had been a milker before he went away and didn't mind what hard work he did, but he couldn't get work for months and months. Him and mother spent pounds on stamps, for they used to send stamped addressed envelopes for any job which was advertised and not many people troubled even to answer their applications.

About this time a Mr David Rice had come to live at Bylaugh Hall. He was an American, and here they wanted servants, so Billy got an indoor job, but only for a few years. There was a lot of talk about the Hall being closed again and eventually it was. So he decided to emigrate to Australia. This was a sad blow to my parents.

BEN

Now about this time Ben, the youngest cripple, left school and it was hoped that Fred, the shoemaker, would teach him the trade, but they couldn't get on. One was slow at learning and the other hadn't the patience, so he was at a loose end. Then Billy Bone, the butcher, asked if he would like to go for a ride on his round with him. This he did, walking on his crutches up Greengate in the morning and walking back in the afternoon. The butcher said this helped him a lot for now he didn't have to stop and tie his horse at every gate. He used to give Ben two-and-six each Christmas. After he had been a week or two on the cart Mr Bone told mother not to pack his lunch for he would get his wife to make him up some sandwiches. All the time he went with him the sandwiches were just bread and dripping, so Mum used to give him something else and our chickens got fat from the dripping sandwiches. After Mr Bone stopped going on the round himself, his wife's nephew came to learn the trade and he used to do the round, and his sandwiches were dripping as well, although he was the butcher's wife's nephew, so Mum packed something for him as well.

Going to the butcher's Ben had to pass High View Farm and used to speak to the three Edwards sons, and then he gradually got to go there to clean knives and forks and boots, etc., not for wages but just for something to pass the time. Then he clipped a lawn and this is where he got into trouble, for my mother going to the shop saw him creeping across the road with a sack of clippings on his shoulder, held in his teeth. She said he was never to do this again for there were cars coming on the roads then, and bicycles. If he did she would stop him from going. Later he kept rabbits and he had to carry things in the same way to them; he would walk on his crutches with the bag in between his teeth and slung across his shoulder.

CRICKET AND AUNT CLARA

Times were changing now and work-people were having Saturday afternoon and bank holidays off from work. A cricket club was formed in the village and the rector lent the rectory meadow, the one toward the RAF station which have the houses built on now. It was next the rectory. The farmers and men played together, the farmers in white trousers, the land workers in their ordinary clothes. At the furthest side of the meadow stood a huge sycamore tree with wide, spreading branches and a table was brought from the back yard of the rectory and tea was served here from a huge urn. The tea had been made in the rectory kitchen and Clara Beevis supervised the serving of it. We were told before we left home not to go near the tea-table because it might embarrass our Aunt Clara, so we always kept to this side of the field. I think if we had gone Clara would have said to us 'What are you doing mor?', for she was a rough diamond with a heart of gold. She and my mother were great friends. Years later my friend Olive took her to catch a train and as they were talking at the carriage door a clergyman came up and said would she mind if he got in the carriage with her? She say 'Lor no bor, there's plenty room for two, git in'.

Murton Webb, who was her husband's boss, left Swanton Morley, for another farm, for at this time the whole village, the estate of the Lombe family, was sold. The farmer took over a place at Knettishall and my uncle went with him as farm steward and Clara did all the book-keeping and money for him because Walter was like my father – they couldn't read or write. The team-man went with them too, the man on the Sunday School outing waggon who drove the horses. They took all their furniture with them, but I think it was only a fortnight before they came back to the same house that he had left.

My sister and I were invited to stay at Knettishall and each morning I went with cousin Jack on the milk float to Thetford. One day Clara said 'You're not going again. You can walk about but your sister cannot get out, so that's that'. I used to take little Dandy the dog and roam the heath near their house.

I saw something on that heath that I never did forget. Dandy and I were ploughing through bracken as high as I was and suddenly at my feet was an open space which looked like a rock-garden. It was about the size of a grave and stones were laid flat on it and grey, green and reddish-brown mosses were growing around and between them in little patches. I always believed that I had walked onto a gypsy grave. It really was beautiful. I did enjoy those walks across the heath.

A VISIT TO WELLS

To come back to the village, people now had bank holidays off work. The train had organized trips to Wells, several during the bank holidays, so villagers talked of going out, perhaps walking into Dereham or to North Elmham station, and then going to Wells. My friend Elsie Wade and I said we would like to go to the sea, but we hadn't the train fare, so we talked it over and said we would bike to Wells. We were told we wouldn't make it but we two felt we could. So we started off in high spirits and we got on fine until we came to the drag at Testerton Hall and there one of us must have wobbled, for the pedals got locked and we landed on the ground. When I got up my foot hurt and I couldn't stand. Oh dear! We didn't want to go back, for we didn't want to be laughed at, so we sat on the bank and at last she said 'Well, we're not far from Horningtoft Hurdle. I'll go and get you a drink'. She brought a soft drink back and said 'This is all I could get, here it is', but I answered 'I cannot see you, where are you?' 'Well', she answered, 'you've got your eyes open'. Well after a time we continued our journey and we got to Wells. She sat me on a seat and went to get some tea. Telling someone in the tent what had happened a member of St. John's came out and he bandaged my foot with his handkerchief. It was rather swollen by this time. During the day I kept soaking it in the sea. We got back safely at night and declared we had had a good day and we were not tired. Well that night I bandaged my ankle in vinegar rags and for a long time I dare not let my mother see me walking. If I knew she was in the district anywhere I would stop, or walk very slowly and she never knew my ankle was black all round. The next time we went to Wells we went by train.

BY PONY AND CART TO NORWICH

As children we were more fortunate than most young people because we had the pony and cart and sometimes went for rides on Sundays. Mostly Ella, Ben and I would go with our parents to Mileham, to our grandparents Ben and Caroline Nichols or to Weasenham Green, for my mother's brother had married my father's sister and they lived there, near the shop owned by Mr Deadman. We sometimes went to another aunt and uncle at Horningtoft.

Father took Ben and Ella, after a thunderstorm, to see a tree and five cows which had been struck with lightning at Elsing, and twice we went on Sunday to Norwich. This was during the first world war. Ben would sit between mother and father, and Ella and I on cushions on the floor at the back in the corners of the cart. The first time we went to hear the band play in Chapel Field gardens and the second time to hear a band at the Salvation Army Citadel in St. Giles. This was of course during the first world war and the service was half-way through when the siren went for an air raid and the service closed and we were out on the street. We were the only people about the streets too, for all had gone to shelter. We had to walk very slowly from St. Giles to Dereham Road where the pony and cart had been left. The landlady of the pub was very good to us and put us in a room facing the street, and when the traffic started again it was a great joy to us to see the trams going by and to hear the ting-ting of the bell. We had taken our own food as usual, but the lady insisted in providing plates. I think my parents had been here often before, for they had taken Fred and Ella to the hospital often, Fred to have his sinews replanted and Ella to have her legs in plaster. This was before I could remember. They were only able to go to the hospital because Mr d'Arcy, for whom father worked, recommended them. Ben had nothing done to his legs. On any trip we went with father he told us all about anything of interest in the district or by the sides of the road.

BY TRAIN TO NORWICH

I also remember going to Norwich about twice by train. What I remember about these outings was the sacks of goods which stood out on the pavement, on The Walk. I believe it was Underwood's grocery. I saw dogs wander up to sacks of beans and nuts and peas and all those kind of things. And on the corner of the flower market was the roast potato and roast chestnut stove. There were metal tub-like barrows which men were pushing about, they had half lift-up lids and they were carrying a broom to sweep up horse dirt where carriages and dray horses had been. And another thing which amused me were the sandwich-board men who walked about the city, sometimes six one behind the other, advertising the theatre; and a very small man who could imitate any kind of bird. He would wander round the streets of Norwich picking up coins as he could.

BACK FROM NORWICH

 Once when I was about fourteen years old mother took us to Norwich by train to see the chrysanthemum show at St. Andrew's Hall. I don't remember how we got to the station, I do know we walked from Dereham station back to Swanton Morley in the evening, for when mother arranged to go, she had forgotten that it was November 5th – fireworks day – and as the pony was nervous of sudden noises Dad would not bring it into Dereham, for young people made big bangs with tins which had a piece of carbide in them. Carbide was the stuff used for bicycle lamps; it gave a wonderful light when water dripped onto it, but it also set light to the lamp often and often.

Ella walked on her crutches all this way, but she was used to walking slowly, for she and Ben would go out when a group of children went, and I can remember them walking up the hill past Pennyspot on the Elsing Road and up the Worthing Road as far as the present RAF station. The other children would wait for them. They also walked to all the meetings at chapel just as often as I went. It was in 1926 when we were living at the other end of the village that they had their first hand-propelled chair. The cripples were all three walking to chapel services twice on Sunday. By evening my sister was raw underneath her arms from using the crutches. A lady, sister to Mrs Goward, who had been a nanny to the Jarrold family in Norwich, wrote to her young boss and he came one Sunday and walked from chapel with them and she, Miss Ayres, had asked him to buy a chair for them, and that is how they became the owners of a chair which they shared.

MAKING AND MENDING

Before going any further I will try and mention the economies which the cottage housewife had to practice.

Sheets when worn in the centre were turned sides into the middles, by seaming the edges and cutting the centre away; or if they were very thin the edges were made into tea-cloths, the very best parts were made into pillow-slips, and the best parts of pillow-slips were made into handkerchiefs.

The best parts of men's vests were cut round and round to make lovely soft bandages, a lot of these were used in our home. Dr. Howlett commented on these saying how good they were, he couldn't think where Mrs Beevis bought them! The tails of the men's shirts were made into dusters, they were mostly blue material. The best parts of worn towels were made into face flannels and dish-cloths. Woollen garments were used for dwiles – floor cloths.

The feet of old socks were made into dannocks – mittens with a thumb, or if the top part of the socks were better, they were cut off and made neat and then sewn between the fingers to make mittens so that fingers were free to use nails and other things. Very old socks were pulled over boots in very slippery weather and deep snow; they kept one from slipping and helped to keep the snow water getting into the leather.

Old spades, when the part near the handle was worn, were put in the ground near a door, upside down, to act as a scraper to clean the mud off boots because there was a lot of mud around. Reading glasses could be bought for sixpence a pair, in any cheap store, you would go and try them on from a stack on the counter and choose the ones you thought you could see best with.

We bought dripping from Bylaugh Hall for fourpence a pound, my father would bring it home and mother would weigh it out, for the neighbours liked this as well.

You could post a letter to someone at 11:30 in the morning and it would be taken into Dereham and be back in Swanton Morley at 1:30 and delivered for a penny stamp. While working in Dereham there was a terrible thunderstorm in the early part of the night. I knew mother would worry about Ella and I, so I walked to the market place just before 12 o'clock at night to post a card and she received it at 7:30 in the morning.

MODERNISATION

I recall seeing the first telephone being erected, and if the wires shook we children thought a message was going along them. They were a good target for the stone throwers, we all tried to hit the white cup on the top.

The first motor car I saw was like two chairs with curved backs. The school inspector, a Mr Addison, had this. I think Dr. Howlett had the next one, he used to drive it up the hill past our yard and go over by the mill. The Bylaugh Hall people had two, one for themselves and visitors, and one for fetching the luggage from Dereham station. Before this they had coaches and horses and a game cart, a kind of shooting brake, for getting the luggage. It was a long vehicle with rails round in light polished wood, driven by Mr Johnson of Bawdeswell. Before these came to Bylaugh we could let our pony out of the stable and just give it a pat and it would go down to the common on its own. It would trot over the hill, past the mill and church, and get there down Mill Street by itself. Now I had to lead it and whatever time I went I seemed to meet one of the motors and the pony would shy.

MORE VILLAGERS

We will go up the hill at the back of the playing field to the mill. If it was a windy day we would see the mill at work with the sails going round and hear it creak, creak as it was grinding corn. In the back office stood two long wooden troughs for making dough and one could watch the baker putting in flour, salt and water at night for next day's bread.

Beyond the bakehouse lived William and Emma Hilton and an adult family – at that time Ernie, Alice, Percy and Dorothy, who would be about sixteen. Later Ernie took over the business. I can only remember Mr Hilton faintly. Mrs Hilton was very deaf and used a black ear trumpet down which we used to shout.

Now from there we will cross the top of the sandpit and come to a double white gate. Most summer afternoons a rather plump old lady would stand here sewing and watching the school children at play. She was the wife of John Howard. Their son, Charlie lived with them, he was a gamekeeper. He would come home in the afternoon with his gun under his arm, and he used to wear brown suede buskins. They had a donkey which was mostly tethered in the lane past the house.

We will go back to the school and perhaps if we are in time we can watch the children go in as the bell ring. They will be in a straight row along the outside wall and will go in one by one.

The next row of cottages are still there – they're next the village hall. An old man past work lived here with his daughter. His name was Ben Leeder. How the children teased him, for his garden ran along the school playground. Next door to the Leeders was my uncle, Walter Beevis, and his wife. He was the shepherd and they had four sons. Clara, his wife, helped to clean the school. Son Jack, went to school for five years without missing and he was given a watch. Each year if you didn't miss one session then you were given a medal, but for five years a watch. Fred and Ella both won medals, both cripples: I didn't.

Now we come up to the back yard, to the corner, and a very old, bent lady lived here. She always wore a thick, black snood on her head, and would take her bread and meat up to the mill bakehouse to be cooked. At the other end of the row was James Brown and his wife Martha.They lived right opposite the village sluice and if we kids got on the wall, Martha would tap on her window and shake her fist at us. James was always smiling. We called him Beggared Brown because he wouldn't say much but when he did he would say 'Beggared so-and-so'.

At the top of Elsing Road lived Stephen and Lizzie Reeve. She had a pretty flower garden and hazelnut bushes were near the gate. She always thought us children were stealing her nuts and her apples. Perhaps we were. Next door, coming down the hill, lived a widow who had two boys, Edwin and Ralph Canham. Opposite their door lived Eddie Trollop. He was a blacksmith, and his wife wore very, very thick glasses. She helped him look after their sows and their little pigs. This is the person who used to send me to shop for two ounces of tea.

My uncle James Beevis and his wife Hannah lived in part of an old farmhouse nearby.

Going up to Greengate are the houses around my home. Mr and Mrs Harris lived in the first house near the road. Then John Lincoln and his wife. He is believed to be related to the Abraham Lincoln family. Joining to their house was Arthur Reeve and Emma, his wife. She once said she had been in a beauty competition, but she was rather old now, not like going in a beauty competition at all. Across the way was George Pearce the shoemaker's house. He had a hut at the top of the garden for his work. Then back to our yard Mrs Golding and the Mace family, and next to us Amelia and Dick Spelman, and then our house. Harris's, Lincoln's, Reeve's and Pearce's houses have all been pulled down. This is where the round house as we call it, the octagonal house, stands now.

Gooseberry Hill is the next port of call, the peculiar house with the one room on the road and the rest on the hill. William and Sarah Beevis, my grandparents, lived here. He was a shepherd, and always wore a smock and carried a crook. Living with them was their daughter Eliza and her husband Starling Jarrett. They had a family, Elsie, Florence, William, Dora, Albert and Ethel.

Now we will have to go up hill for a walk to the Barracks, but first we shall have to pass a deep pit of water whose overflow passed down the hill and past our house to the sluice. In winter time us children used to slide on here, crowds of us. I wonder we were not drowned for the ice would crack and the boys would shout 'Crack she bears then she breaks'. Next to this big pit there was an orchard, an apple orchard, belonging to the farm on the other side of the road. The Barracks was a row of small houses which have since been pulled down and bungalows built on the site. In the first two lived old Lee Harris and his wife Laura; they had two of these houses because they had several in the family. Old Lee was the roadman and on Saturday afternoons he was the village barber. I used to have to push Ben here in his chair to have his hair cut, and Laura would be bringing huge pies out of the oven, which was in the same room as they were cutting the hair, and the old men would mardle and mardle as I stood waiting for Ben to take his turn.

At the top of Greengate a shop stood out in the road. It was just a shop at that time, later it was the Post Office and has only been pulled down this last few years and a new post office built. George Rix lived here. He was a very old man, leaning on a stick, with white hair and a white, flowing beard. He always carried sweets in his pocket to give to any children he saw on the road.

Near The Limes, the house by the chapel, the one with the clock on the front, lived Mr Billy Butters and his wife. She was so house-proud that he had to take his boots off on the doorstep, and she wrapped all the table- and chair-legs with newspaper for fear they should get scratched.

Now to Pond Farm, so named because there was a big pond on the opposite side of the road where Bedingfield houses are now and a wide ditch of water at the side. Mr and Mrs Johnson lived here and farmed the land. Mr Johnson was a big man. He looked rather like Clement Freud, the Liberal man, and his wife was small. She went to church every Sunday morning and I would see her reading her bible near the bedroom window on weekdays. Her windows were packed with cyclamens, every year, huge big ones, windows full of them. Their younger son, Bertie, went to the first world war and lost one leg.

Now to the long white house which is endways to the road where Mr Pigg lived. He used to drive a donkey and cart and would go on Sundays to the Brethren meetings at Bawdeswell. His daughter used to walk to Dereham, to the Salvation Army hall, and James Pearce, her husband, used to come to the Methodist chapel. I heard Phillip Pigg say once that his daughter would never get up till his wife had the breakfast on the table. She listened to hear the cups rattle first; so one morning Phillip went into the pantry and rattled the cups, making quite a noise, and Bessie got up but no breakfast was ready.

In their yard was a small old apple tree; the fruit had pink streaks from the top to the bottom. How do I know this? Well, there was a swing on that tree and we used to try it when the apples were ripe.

Now we come to the Angel. Mr and Mrs Tye lived here. Miss Maggie Tye, the school-teacher, was one of their daughters. Pat Tye, who was the postman, was a son. For many years he was postman in the village.

Next came the police house. The police used to ride bicycles in those days and meet their neighbour from the next village at night. No-one ever knew where they were and they'd just give the boys a box of the ears if they found them doing anything wrong.

Now to come to our house where we live now, Benella, so-named after my cripple brother Ben and sister Ella. Nikey Ayers lived here. He kept a pony and cart and housed the pony in the wash-house. At the other end of the house lived a Mr and Mrs Adcock. They had a donkey and cart and sold lettuces and strawberries which they grew themselves. Earlier they used to go round with herrings and sell.

Now we are back near the church by an L-shaped row of houses. Round the corner lived my uncle George and Aunt Sarah, but they moved to a farm in North Tuddenham and Ernest and Harriet Reeve took their house over. It only had one large room with a window to the street and a door in the yard. His name was Twosticks. Harriet was real broad Norfolk and her children Berty and Gertie she called Barty and Gartie.

Zephaniah Jarvis and his wife lived in The Dial for many years and their daughter, Violet. He said once his wife talked so much he bought her peanuts to keep her quiet. Next is the School House where Mr and Mrs Weaver lived, with a servant. The School House was black beams and white plaster at this time.

We shall have to pass the sluice on the Brown's corner and walk round this to the blacksmith's shop where we shall come to those two huge horse-chestnut trees and if it's autumn time we shall be slipping around under inches of leaves for they were never swept up.

Now farther along, opposite where the other Barracks were, was another row of three houses. These were called Barracks as well. In the middle of this row lived the family of Thomas Brooks, father and mother. They always called her 'Ria' Brooks. I don't know what her name was but she was always 'Ria' Brooks. There was Billy and Tom and Annie and Joe and Dorothy and Jimmy and Reggie and Denny. Mrs Brooks used to bring babies into the world for other people too and also prepared the dead for departure.

Higher up lived the Hudson family. They kept cows and he came round with cockles and mussels in his horse and cart, and sometimes herring. Next door was occupied by Walter Bone and Sarah, his wife. They had cows as well and a pony or horse – I believe two horses – for he did the allotment ploughing.

There was a farm at the corner of Woodgate where the Easter family lived and Charity Farm was opposite. A cousin of mine, Herbert Beevis, lived here and worked for Mr Easter. Further on we will go down the little loke which leads to Frog's Hall. At the bend in the road were two houses. One of these was occupied by Mr and Mrs Myhill, Herbert, Rosie, Madge and Connie. They used to bring bunches of violets to school, for the banks were full of them down there.

NICKNAMES

Now most people had nicknames. I will mention a few, the first will be the nickname and the second the surname. Char Smith, Duro Pegg, Thingo Cooper, Dido Brookes, Forerunner Beevis, Chalky Canham, Tin Plates, Bismark Beevis, Biddy Beevis, Two-sticks Reeve, Attoe Marsh, Pongo Marsh, Byla Reeve, Tory Gaff, Glimp Pegg, Hooligan Mitchell, Beggared Brown, Sparrow Rump, Willow Marsh, Billy Sort Beevis, Little Arthur and Little Ann Reeve, Nissy Hudson and Snism Hudson, Mother Lapstone Smith, Bruiser Howard, Pet Howard, Clipper Anderson, Lefry Beevis, Jay Mitchell, Polly Bunker Rawlings, Sancho Panza Cooper, Ruddy Seaman, Jolter Peachment, Bubbles Anderson, Nikey Ayres, Tibbo Reeve and Biff Reeve, Smiler Hudson and Dodo Barry.

FINALLY

I couldn't close this without saying what very good parents we had. Oh, my mother kept us in order all right and had a little twig to tickle us sometimes and for the older boys she had a rubber golosh, and gave them a hiding with it.

We never did hear our parents quarrel or even argue with one another. Whatever differences they had they must have settled quietly. Neither did they upset us with their grief when they lost both sets of parents in a few months, nor at the time their eldest son was killed. They never swore, smoked or drank strong drink, home made stout was made in the home and used. We had a wonderful contented home life although they had no money. I remember mother saying once they were reduced to only one pound in the whole world.

My father never did hit one of us children, in all his life he was very quiet and kind.

MR. HOPSON'S MEDICAL CLUB,

held at *Dail Inn Swanton*

Name *Mrs Golding*

1870 2	Pd/1s	Pd/1s	Pd/1s	Pd/1s
1871 3	Pd/1s	Pd/1s	Pd/1s	Pd/1s
1872 4	Pd/1s	Pd/1s	Pd/1s	Pd/1s
1873 5	Pd 1/3	Pd 1/3	Pd 1/3	Pd 1/3

Children under the age of 10 to pay 3d. per quarter.
Above that age and under 16 6d. ,,
All persons above the age of 16 1s. ,,

NOTICE.

This Card is intended solely for the benefit of such of the Poor and Labouring Classes as are not entitled, or may not desire to receive Medical Relief from the Parish; and it is to be distinctly understood, that no persons will be admitted into the Club, except those who have no other means of obtaining Medical aid.

Patients requiring Medicine or Attendance, must make application at the Surgery between 9 and 10 o'clock in the morning, and provide themselves with Bottles.

THIS CARD MUST ALWAYS BE BROUGHT.

Mrs Betsy Golding, Daisy's landlady, paid her doctor quarterly for medical care for herself and her family. In 1870, adults paid a shilling (5p); by 1910 this had gone up to 3/6 (17½p) - 3½ times as much